Gertrude Reinisch

Wanda Rutkiewicz

A Caravan of Dreams

Translated from German by Dieter Pevsner

Carreg

Contents

Moon-gilded Mountains

When I first saw
The mountains
I was twenty-six.
I neither laughed
Nor cried,
But in their presence
I spoke in whispers.
At home once more
I tried
To tell my mother
The look of the mountains.
Not an easy task.
Everything
Is so different in the night,
Mountains and words.
Mother kept silence,
Asleep, perhaps.
The moon waxed among the clouds,
The poor man's gilded mountain.

Tadeusz Rozewicz

Carreg Ltd, 18 Parsons Croft, Hildersley, Ross-on-Wye, Hereford, HR9 5BN

First published in English by Carreg Ltd in 2000

Translated from Wanda Rutkiewicz – Karawane der Träume by Gertrude Reinisch
First published 1998 by Bergverlag Rudolf Rother GmbH, Munich

© Bergverlag Rudolf Rother GmbH, Munich 1998
English translation © Carreg Ltd 2000

Gertrude Reinisch has asserted her moral rights of paternity and integrity under the Copyright, Designs and Patents Act 1988

ISBN 0 9538631 0 7

Picture credits:
Willi Bauer: half-title portrait, pp. 23, 35 upper and lower, 38, 73, 78 upper and lower, 83, 84 lower, 86, 87
Mikolaj Blaskiewicz: pp. 14/15
Frieder Blickle/Bilderberg-Archiv der Fotografen: p. 149
Marion Feik: p. 144 upper
Leo Graf: pp. 26 lower, 27 lower, 31 upper, 51 upper, 102 right
Sigi Hupfauer: pp. 44, 45 upper, 46 upper
Kurt Lyncke: p. 113 lower
Herbert Mayerhofer: p. 165 upper
Joachim Moritz: pp. 20/21, 22 lower
Wolfgang Nairz:: pp. 90, 91 upper and lower, 92/93
Karl Ölmüller: pp. 70 upper and lower, 71
Gertrude Reinisch: pp. 1, 2/3, 4/5, 6/7, 8/9, 12/13, 33 lower, 40/41, 42, 54, 55 upper and lower, 56, 57, 58, 59, 60 upper and lower, 61, 80/81, 89, 99 upper, 100 upper and lower, 105 upper and lower, 107, 108 lower, 109 upper and lower, 110 lower, 111, 112, 114, 116 upper and lower, 117 upper and lower, 120 upper and lower, 121, 122, 123 upper and lower, 124, 125, 127, 128/129, 131, 133, 134 lower, 135, 136, 138/139, 143 upper, 151, 152, 154/155, 161 upper and lower, 162, 167, 168/169, 170 upper, 174, 175, 176 lower, 182, 186/187, 188/189
Willi Ruprecht: p. 28 lower
Anneliese Scharbl: p. 31 lower left and right
All other photographs: Bilder Archiv Wanda Rutkiewicz

The poem on p. 9, Moon-gilded Mountains by Tadeusz Rozewicz, appears by permission of Anvil Press Poetry Ltd.

Printed in the United Kingdom by Butler & Tanner Ltd, Frome & London.

Distributed in North America by AlpenBooks, Mukilteo, WA 98275.

Foreword

Wanda Rutkiewicz was the finest woman alpinist in the world, a charismatic person and a stronger, more accomplished climber than many men. She climbed with twenty expeditions spread over 22 years. But on 12 May 1992 she vanished without trace at 8300 metres while attempting to add Kanchenjunga to the eight 8000-metre peaks she had already climbed.

Even now, so long after the event, her friends find it hard to believe that she will not be returning from that last climb. We were thoroughly accustomed to the long gaps between the brief, unannounced visits when she happened to be passing between expeditions. Wanda lived in the fast lane, and few of us could keep up with her: hence the intensity of the joy and the tragedy that she packed into her short life.

She left us a rich legacy – in the form of diaries, audio tapes, videos, reels of unedited film, photographs, and transparencies often in mis-labelled mounts. All this she had put by against the day when she would have written this book, had she been able to find time during her sojourn in the world. It has fallen to me to play the detective and try to put some order into this mass of material. I am very conscious that the result is not free of error.

This book will not answer all the questions about Wanda. She never answered them herself and I was determined not to fictionalize. She always hoped that people who wrote about her would write what she said, not what they thought. Even where I am recording events that we shared, I have tried to distinguish unequivocally between her perspective and my own.

My love and respect were for the real, flesh-and-blood Wanda, with all her passion, her strengths and her weaknesses, not for some invented, mythic heroine. I never felt drawn to the flatterers who fawned on Wanda to her face while savaging her behind her back. I deeply admired her: for her achievements, her battling spirit and her stamina. And when I disagreed with her, I told her so. Our friendship was always honest, and it is my wish and hope that this book should be no less honest.

I am grateful to the many women and men who helped this book to the light of day: Marion Feik, who fostered the project through every stage as though it were her own; Wanda's family and especially her nephew Micolaj Blaskiewicz, the curator of Wanda's archive; Ewa Panieko-Pankiewicz, Wanda's favourite climbing partner; the many expedition climbers who made photographs available; Tatjana Gregoritsch, who found a publisher, in Bergverlag Rother, willing to produce a book of a quality worthy of the finest woman mountaineer the world has known; Leo Graf, for his invaluable help and advice; a friend who prefers not to be named but without whose timely interventions this book might never have been completed; Walter Theil, Publisher and Managing Director of Bergverlag Rother, Annette Köhler, my editor, and Klaus Wolfsperger, whose design has made this book a thing of beauty.

Gertrude Reinisch

A brief childhood

1943–1964

4 February 1943	Wanda Rutkiewicz born at Plungiany, Lithuania
1946	Sister born, move to Wroclaw (Breslau)
1948	Elder brother killed
1949	Younger brother born
1949–1959	School
1959–1964	Mechanical and Electrical Engineering studies and degree at Warsaw Polytechnic
1964	Elected Polytechnic's Sportsman of the Year Selected for Olympic volleyball team North wall of Mnich

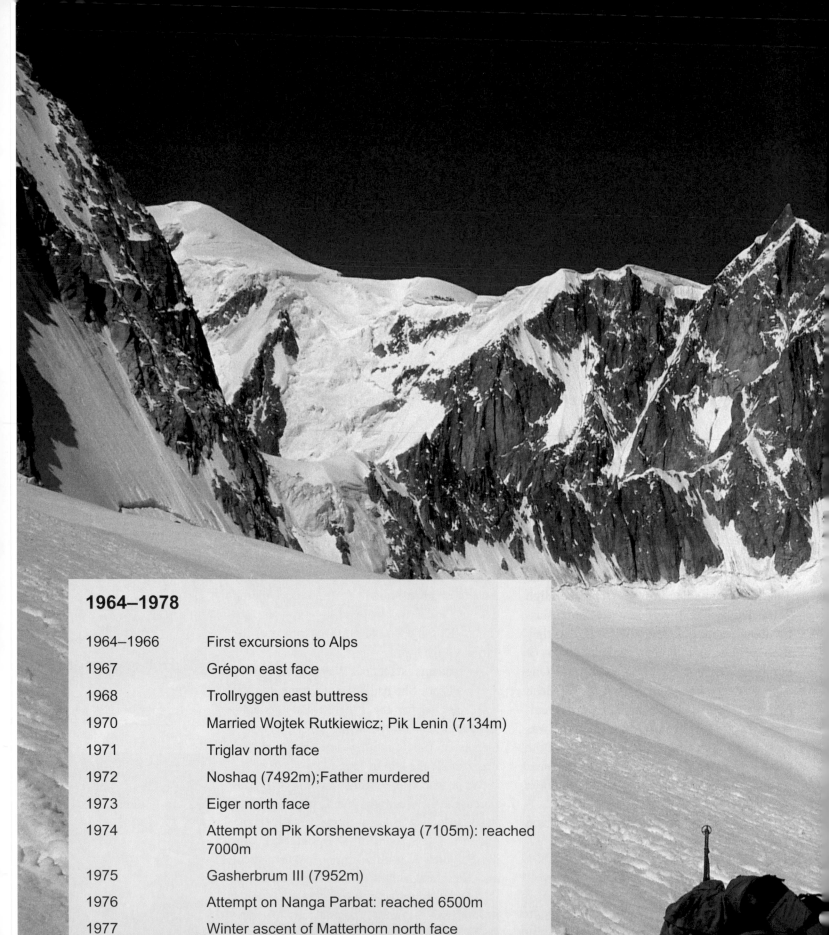

1964–1978

1964–1966	First excursions to Alps
1967	Grépon east face
1968	Trollryggen east buttress
1970	Married Wojtek Rutkiewicz; Pik Lenin (7134m)
1971	Triglav north face
1972	Noshaq (7492m);Father murdered
1973	Eiger north face
1974	Attempt on Pik Korshenevskaya (7105m): reached 7000m
1975	Gasherbrum III (7952m)
1976	Attempt on Nanga Parbat: reached 6500m
1977	Winter ascent of Matterhorn north face

Paths to Freedom

First encounter with the Alps

Wanda's first opportunity to climb in the Alps came in 1964 when it was still a formidable business to organize all the necessary invitations and authorizations for such a trip. Her invitation came from an Austrian volleyball club whose members she had met at a tournament in Poland. No sooner had she crossed the Iron Curtain – with $20 in her pocket for a six-weeks' stay, a rucksack full of food, a Zorki camera and an amber necklace given her by her mother – than she went down with a soaring temperature.

Her arm was hugely swollen, and she was found to have a septic cyst, probably infected during a working visit to Leningrad where she had foolishly gone for a swim in a lake marked 'Danger. Polluted Water'.

She was forced to break her journey in Innsbruck to get the cyst lanced – as luck would have it, by Dr Helmut Scharfetter. She spent her convalescence with him, climbing in the Zillertal Alps and taking a mountain rescue course.

She returned to the Alps in 1965, again climbing with Dr Scharfetter. But he was now too deeply committed to his surgeon's profession to have much time to spare for the peaks.

Wanda made a third trip to the Alps in 1966. She arrived with even heavier rucksacks, full of climbing equipment and food for a month. What little money she had went only on stamps and bread. 'I couldn't afford ski lifts or cable cars. I climbed under my own steam from the very foot of Mont Blanc to the summit. How many metres' ascent and descent is that? In fact I did it several times, and it must have been almost as strenuous as some of my later climbs in the Himalayas. I fell under the spell of the French Alps, but I also acquired a lasting hatred for climbing with heavy loads.'

In 1967 Wanda was in the French Alps again, with Halina Krüger-Syrokomska. They did not know one another, but had both been selected by the Wysokogórsk Alpine Club, who had insured them, paid their railway tickets and given them $70 allowance for a month's stay. It was the kind of opportunity that every Polish climber, male or female, dreamed of. Halina, three years older than Wanda, was a popular climber and already had some very severe routes to her credit. But she would need a partner, and Wanda was chosen for her experience of the Alps. 'I was so grateful to the club for supporting us women climbers, and ecstatic to be doing what so many others were dreaming of.'

The two women started with a traverse of Mont Blanc and an ascent of the Grépon east face as a prelude to an attempt on the Bonatti pinnacle – one of the most difficult routes in

Grand Capucin from the Petit Capucin

▶ *Mont Blanc and the Peuterey Ridge from the North*

22

the Alps. The usual approach at that time, and the most dangerous part of the whole ascent, was up the Dru couloir, an ice channel that is continually bombarded by rock- and ice-falls. If you fail to make the summit of the Bonatti pinnacle, you have to turn round and brave the couloir all over again. That is exactly what happened to Halina and Wanda when the weather turned against them.

Their attempt on the Grands Charmoz was halted by an electric storm, and an unexpected change in the weather also foiled their climb on the Grand Capucin. In almost continuous lightning and deafening howling wind and thunder the two women could barely communicate. They had to abseil into the void under the overhangs of the west face. The mist made route-finding difficult; they could only hope to plot the right course to

each of the following abseil points. 'We were wet through and very cold. We were abseiling in Dülfer slings. At one point Halina's hood got tangled with the rope and nearly strangled her. Luckily we kept our nerve, stayed cool and came out of this little episode unharmed. It was another ten years before I made it to the top of the Grand Capucin.'

The same year Wanda fell 18 metres off a face on the Skalki. By then, fortunately, her back muscles were so strong that her spine was undamaged, and she was climbing again in a mere two weeks.

Polish politics profoundly influenced Wanda's life. Her parents were perpetually short of money. Her father had registered seven patents connected with his work and expertise, but the substantial return that he was counting on never materialized. He lived in some private, inaccessible world of his own, lost in dreams of emigrating to South America, even learning Spanish against that day. It was only her mother's tireless efforts that kept the household together, yet her father was always wanting her to go out to work.

'Maybe my parents' relationship was so unhappy because they were always short of money, but I think there must have been a deeper reason which they kept from us children.' When her father left home (when Wanda was 25) her parents fought over who should have the dreary terrace house. Finally Wanda bought it with a bank loan so as to make the family independent of her father.

'We had some rules in the family, but there was space for each of us to find our individual ways. I would have taken any attempt to limit my independence as a personal attack.' Wanda never discussed personal matters at home. Her style was to operate by reason and logic, whereas her mother lived by yoga and the metaphysical. And yet when Wanda needed to confide in someone, she would turn to her mother, while always keeping the channels open to her father.

Adventure on the east buttress of the Trollryggen

In 1968 Halina and Wanda travelled to Norway with a group of Polish climbers. The Norwegian peaks are only about 2500 metres high, but ascents begin virtually at sea level. The rock face of Trollryggen – 1600 metres from bottom to top – is one of the most impressive in Europe. Because any ascent must reckon with several nights bivouacked on the face, climbers have to carry a heavy load of equipment and food – and, most especially, of water.

Wanda and Halina were the first women's team to climb on the east buttress. To save weight, they decided against carrying a stove, taking only drinking water and lemonade powder. Their main difficulty was finding the route up the colossal wall to the summit, as the weather, and visibility, turned against them after the first day. 'It was very exciting. We bivouacked twice on the rock and

reached the summit on the third day. It was a wonderful climb. Norway is magnificent in July – with just four hours of darkness between the long days.'

'We were even interviewed for a cover story in Playboy. We were photographed standing on some random pile of stones nowhere near Trollryggen – and with all our clothes on, unlike all the other women in the magazine.'

However, Wanda's Norwegian excursion was not an unqualified success. She took a fall while negotiating a rock overhang, hit one leg on a rock projection, breaking her ankle, and arrived back in Poland with her leg in plaster. But she soon got bored and hobbled off on her crutches to the granite crags of Skalki. 'I had myself tied to the rope and climbed some Grade IV routes. I avoided putting weight on my foot by supporting the weight against my knee. This is normally considered most improper because, of course, you're only ever supposed to use your hands and feet.' As usual, Wanda went on climbing after everyone else had decided to stop, and ended up having to run across a field – on her crutches – to catch the train home.

The route up the 1600 metres of the east buttress of the Trollryggen starts almost at sea level.

First expeditions to a wider world

Wanda at her marriage to Wojtek Rutkiewicz

Pik Lenin base camp

'Honeymoon' on Pik Lenin, 7134 m

In April 1970 Wanda Blaszkiewicz married Wojtek Rutkiewicz, a mathematician and the son of Poland's deputy minister for health, whom she had met climbing. That summer she leaped at the opportunity, her first, to join an expedition. 'The trip settled the fate of my marriage. In effect, I was taking myself on honeymoon, and Wojtek felt bitterly hurt.' The expedition was to Pik Lenin (7134m), and comprised a selected group of Poles and a team from Novosibirsk. From the outset Wanda felt unhappy as the only woman in the group, but she knew that the chance was too good to miss. 'We all had to work together, which made for some problems which I had never encountered in the Tatra or the Alps where I was climbing with people I knew and understood. And the preparations were so complicated that it took an age to get to any climbing. Even when we got to Pik Lenin we seemed to be just stomping around in the snow for several weeks. Admittedly I got my first 7000-metre peak out of it, but it was years before I learned to find any personal rewards in this kind of climbing. When I got home from the Pamirs, I swore never to join another expedition.'

It took Wanda another year to find a job in Warsaw – at the Institute of Mathematical

Computing – so as to be able to join her husband. But Wojtek had none of Wanda's fanatical obsession with climbing and found her unusual ambitions too much at odds with his own more conventional ideas about marital roles.

'I always took anything that might limit my independence as a personal attack, to be resisted rather than accommodated in any way ...' So she divorced after only three years. She kept her married name of Rutkiewicz – '... whatever the name, I'm still the same person ...' – but she never saw Wojtek again. He re-married and has a family.

Overland to Afghanistan
Travelling to faraway countries was no more than a rosy dream for most Poles in the 1960s and 1970s. If you were lucky enough to be selected for an expedition, you would unhesitatingly thrust all possible obstacles aside, forget your family, and arrange to take leave from your job. In the Soviet bloc both the State and other institutions, businesses and factories regularly sponsored expeditions and allowed you to take leave without losing pay. The Polish Alpine Association had a Himalayan fund which was subsidized by the National Committee for Physical Education and Tourism. Every three years the Ministry of Sport funded so-called National Expeditions of Poland's best climbers, for which it made available all the necessary foreign currencies as well as zlotys. The members of each expedition were selected by an expedition leader sitting with the so-called Sporting Committee of the Alpine Association. However, individual clubs were permitted to raise money locally and mount expeditions of their own. For example, members might use their special skills to take on dangerous jobs and pay their earnings into their club's expedition fund.

The 1970s saw many such Polish expeditions travel out into the world. Some were put to secondary use in surveying and cartography; some were partly financed by wealthy Poles in the West. Whatever the sources of the money, one certainty was that the expedition members themselves could never have raised even their plane tickets out of their own savings. At that time most Polish Himalayan expeditions travelled overland, by train, to Afghanistan, because that was the cheapest way. Tickets to their destination of Termez were not available, so they would have to book on to Dushanbe but get off at Termez, take the ferry across the Amur-Dario, and then continue by truck. A good alternative was to fly from Termez to Tashkent or direct to Kabul because the Tashkent–Kabul section could be paid in zlotys, making the price less than a month's Polish average earnings. Up to 1979, when the Russians withdrew from Afghanistan and the country fell into civil war, over 100 Polish expeditions had climbed in the Hindu Kush.

At ease in the Pik Lenin base camp

Pik Lenin, Camp III

1978–1990

1978	Mount Everest (8848m)
1979	Grand Capucin east face; Petit Dru west face
1981	Elbrus in winter; complex leg fracture – $2^{1}/_{2}$ years on crutches
1982	Married Dr Helmut Scharfetter; Austrian citizenship; Rolex Enterprise Award; leader of women's K2 expedition
1984	Attempt on K2, reaching 7400m; attempt on Broad Peak, reaching 7150m; separation from Dr Helmut Scharfetter
1985	Return to Warsaw; Aconcagua South Face (6959m); Nanga Parbat (8125m), second attempt on Broad Peak, reaching 7800m
1986	K2 (8616m); third attempt on Broad Peak; attempt on Makalu, reaching 8000m; meeting with Dr Marion Feik, who becomes Wanda's manager
1987	Attempt on Annapurna (8091m) in winter, reaching 7000m; Shisha Pangma (8046m); attempt on Cerro Torre
1988	Raichle Adventure Prize; Yosemite; attempt on Yalung Kang
1989	Victor de l'aventure Award, France; Gasherbrum II (8035m)
1990	Match d'or, Paris; Minerva della donna, Italy; second attempt on Makalu; Hidden Peak (8068m); death of Wanda's friend Kurt Lyncke on Broad Peak

8000-metre peaks

Paths to adventure

Mount Everest

To the summit of the world

Wanda was now ranked with the world's top women climbers. Her winter climb of the north face of the Matterhorn in such appalling conditions turned out to have been a dress rehearsal for an assault on the world's highest peak. In 1978 Dr Herrligkoffer began to assemble a Franco–German Everest expedition (including also a number of Austrian and Swiss climbers). He not only invited Wanda to join, but even remitted her 6000 Marks membership fee in exchange for a contribution in the form of Polish equipment.

'Realizing that normally-funded expeditions cost them far more, the Polish Alpine Association were quick to agree to these terms. And I didn't anticipate any problems on the expedition, even though there were then very few German women climbers of sufficient calibre to lead or take decisions.'

Herrligkoffer was to lead the German group, Pierre Mazeaud the French, and the plan was to climb from Nepal by the same route as the first ascent, up the tumbling towers and the perilous crevasses of the Khumbu Icefall that hangs between the flanks of Everest and Lhotse. It is the classic route and most expeditions favour it.

Mountaineers regard this 'normal route' as straightforward: the technical difficulties are moderate and climbers have no need of exceptional rock- or ice-climbing skills, but ascents are still fraught with other dangers. Weather changes are as frequent as they are

Wanda in her apartment, packing for Everest

Mount Everest, 8848m, called Chomolungma ('Mother Goddess of the Snows') in Tibetan, has always attracted the lion's share of attention among the Himalayan giants. British mountaineers made repeated attempts on the highest mountain on earth from the early 20th century.

In March 1922 Mallory and his companions reached 8225m without oxygen. Capt. Finch and his partner Capt. Bruce, with oxygen masks, reached 8320 m. On the third summit attempt, an avalanche dragged three British climbers and fourteen Sherpas down the face, killing seven of the Sherpas.

Two years later another British expedition again attacked the mountain from the north. On 8 June 1924 George Leigh Mallory and Andrew Irvine set out from Camp VI (8540m) for the summit. About noon another expedition member saw two dots moving close to the summit, but cloud closed in soon after and the two climbers were never seen again.

Every subsequent expedition for almost 30 years, including a Soviet group in 1952, failed.

Finally, on 29 May 1953 Edmund Hillary, an apiculturist from New Zealand, and Sherpa Tensing Norgay from Darjeeling climbed by way of the South Col to stand on the roof of the world. Tenzing laid chocolate and sweetmeats in the snow to appease the gods. The two men had realized every mountaineer's dream.

In 1963 a large-scale American expedition led by N.G. Dyhrenfurth achieved the first traverse of the mountain.

In 1975 an expedition of 14 Japanese women attempted the peak, and Junko Tabei became the first woman to reach the summit. Not many days later Phantong, from Tibet, became the second woman to make the summit – by the North Ridge, together with eight men, all nine being members of the second major Chinese Everest expedition. All but one of the prin-cipal climbers on this Chinese expedition were Tibetans.

During the 1978 Austrian Expedition led by Wolfgang Nairz, Reinhold Messner and Peter Habeler made the first ascent by the South-east Ridge, without oxygen. Nine climbers reached the summit, including the first German, Reinhard Karl.

In the same year K.M. Herrligkoffer and P. Mazeaud's Franco–German expedition put 16 climbers on the summit, including Wanda Rutkiewicz, who thus became the first European woman and the third world-wide to succeed.

In 1979 a Yugoslav expedition opened a route up the length of the hitherto unclimbed West Ridge.

In 1980 a Polish expedition made the first winter ascent; a Japanese group climbed the full height of the North Face; another Polish expedition made the first ascent of the South Buttress; and Reinhold Messner made the first solo ascent of Everest, partly by a new route.

In 1995 Nepal instituted a fee of $50,000 per expedition, in the hope of reducing the traffic on the mountain.

unpredictable, the risks on the Khumbu Ice Fall are beyond calculation and sheer altitude makes oxygen deficiency inevitable.

'Everest challenges you to overcome the cold, the weather, snow, ice, rock, exhaustion and your own fears; and those challenges face every climber equally and on every ascent. To hope to reach the summit you need a lot of knowledge and a lot of different skills.'

Most of the expedition members hardly knew one another, and many were not best pleased when Herrligkoffer appointed Wanda assistant deputy leader (with Sigi Hupfauer as the deputy).

'The other members made it very clear that a woman's place was anywhere but on an alpine expedition; but I'm my own person and I'm never prepared to be treated as just

Camp I with Lhotse behind

any young woman. The men were against me from the beginning. They had never encountered my kind of independence before, and they couldn't bring themselves to accept me as an equal partner. Unfortunately there are certain kinds of male groups who perceive any collaboration on equal terms with women as a threat to their masculinity. My style was very different from theirs, and when the two were in conflict their response was aggression.

'As a woman you're more likely to be asked on to an expedition for being the wife of another member than for your alpine skills. How can women's climbing ever win proper respect when every woman on every mixed expedition is continuously judged by the men, and driven to prove herself better than them? That kind of pressure to perform and achieve only increases the risks.

'The problems might not have escalated so bitterly if I had had it in me to be sweeter or more diplomatic, but I'm no good at pretending and I won't sink to feminine wiles. I suppose "proper women" defuse conflicts by quiet diplomacy, whereas I simply withdraw into myself and pursue my own purposes.'

Herrligkoffer wrote his own account of the conflict. 'On 6 September there was a falling out the like of which I had never experienced on any of my many expeditions. The root of the trouble was the perceived discrepancy between Wanda's emancipated and self-confident attitude and her inability to share tasks and burdens equally with her male colleagues. The discussion deteriorated into the most naked display of unfeeling masculine selfishness that I have ever witnessed ...'

Wanda was supposed to shoot film, and that created more problems. 'The men thought it would let me match their achievements but for less effort, so I felt I had to be constantly proving my independence of them by climbing unroped, even up the ice-fall. It was the same down in base camp, where my style and my ideas – and the fact that I'm not prepared to accept traditional

The climbers' group in the Khumbu Icefall

women's roles – seemed to be for ever generating conflicts and aggression.'

The second summit group was to consist of three Sherpas and four expedition members, and Herrligkoffer insisted that Wanda should be one of them. The first summit group had already been successful and halted overnight at Camp IV when the second group set out. Wanda had not included a sleeping bag in her load but Kurt Diemberger passed her his – and only those who have actually sat through a night at -40°C can fully appreciate his generosity.

But on 16 October, when the group, starting from the South Col, had reached 8400m and Sigi Hupfauer ordered Wanda to carry an additional oxygen bottle up a further 100 metres, Wanda protested: 'I'm already carrying my film equipment.' Sigi exploded in rage. 'The others simply climbed away, leaving me standing, searching desperately in the snow for my oxygen bottle. Panic gripped me; my knees were trembling and I shouted after my colleagues as they disappeared. I felt

I had hit rock bottom. What was the point of battling to conquer the mountain if it meant unleashing such violent hatreds and aggressions? But then Sherpa Mingma called out that he had the bottle and I knew I couldn't give up, so I summoned up the last of my reserves …'

Later in 1978 Sigi Hupfauer was to write, 'Dorje and Mingma carried oxygen for Wanda to the South Summit! I suppose no

Wanda in the top camp on the South Col, wearing her oxygen mask

45

'... I was just happy, as anyone would have been at that moment ...' Wanda at the summit with Willi Klimek

'... I could feel how close I was to the summit and I was ecstatic. The growing feeling that nothing can stop you is just marvellous.' Wanda on the Hillary Step, the crux just below the summit

woman would have a serious chance of reaching a summit this high without help of this kind ...' About the same time, Wanda wrote, 'I had a very strange feeling in the pit of my stomach when I realized that I was alone at this altitude ... My worst fear was that, if I fell, no one would even notice.'

She followed the men's tracks through the deep snow and balanced, unroped, along the icy ridge between the South Col and the Hillary Step. Snow and ice was cascading continuously down the steep slopes on either side into the depths 1000 metres below. Fortunately Willi shouted across to remind her to film the scene.

'Suddenly my air cut out and I tore my oxygen mask off, but when I saw the others on the summit, nothing could stop me. At 2 p.m., just 15 minutes after the others, I was

on the highest point on earth, living proof that we are all capable of more than we think. When I looked around me, I thought I could actually see the curvature of the globe. I had brought a little stone up with me that I had picked up and kept on my first climbing day in Poland, and I pushed it down into the snow at the very summit. Sigi congratulated me, adding that personal differences counted for nothing at the top of Everest ... He cleaned out the ice that had blocked my oxygen filter and I felt a deep happiness, a sense that the group had become my brothers, and a fresh appreciation of everything around me.'

Wanda was more concerned about the way down than the ascent. 'It's absolutely essential to keep one step ahead of yourself because most accidents are the result of stupidity. I took the greatest care with every step, and kept reminding myself of all the friends I had lost in the mountains. I even talked aloud to myself non-stop, saying things like "Careful, now!" to make sure that I made no false moves. I was probably suffering from altitude sickness.'

But when she got back to base camp, Wanda found that nothing had changed in the men's attitude to her, and she was happy to leave the expedition as quickly as she could. After the Everest expedition she found it

more and more difficult to understand how women could go on tolerating the unpleasantnesses of working with men, rather than learning to organize themselves collectively. 'Of course I can see that it's easier for a woman in a mainly masculine team to notch up achievements at the limits of her own capacities, and that's why I have more respect for the best achievements of all-women teams where the members can demonstrate what they are truly capable of …'

When she got back to Kathmandu, Wanda found a report waiting for her from Arlene Blum, the leader of an American women's expedition to Annapurna which had assembled just a couple of months before, in August 1978. Wanda knew Arlene from the Noshaq expedition, and another member of the Annapurna team, Alison Chadwick-Onyszkiewicz, from Gasherbrum.

Two women and two Sherpas had made the summit of Annapurna on 15 October – just one day before Wanda had stood on the summit of Everest. Alison, who had always insisted that '… this whole Annapurna venture will be meaningless unless we can take the summit ourselves, without any Sherpas', was teamed up with Vera Watson to make the second attempt.

Arlene's report continued: 'That evening we couldn't raise Vera and Alison on the radio and we began to feel very uneasy. What were we all doing risking our lives just to stand on the top of a mountain? We couldn't pick up any trace of them that day or the next, and only found their bodies several days later. Had they fallen? Been knocked off the face by a rock- or ice-fall? All we knew was how shocked we were by the tragedy and what a deep shadow it cast over all the other memorable experiences we women had shared on this, our own expedition. The one positive lesson of their deaths, if there could be one, was that we should learn to distinguish the important elements in our lives, and concentrate on them to the exclusion of all else.'

Wanda was now the first European woman to have stood on the summit of the world, the third woman ever, a member of the 30th summit team and the 78th member of the entire human race. 'I've certainly never scoffed at the mythic aura surrounding Everest, or at the magic of its sheer might. That's why I carried that tiny bit of Poland – my nursery-slopes rock – to the top, and brought a little piece of the South Summit home to Poland. I can't say that my memories of Everest are very happy, but it is the highest peak of all and it demands our respect. It is the home of the Gods.'

Wanda was brought up as a Catholic and she never lost her faith. 'A lot of the people who need ritual and parrot the forms and phrases of liturgy have long since forgotten

Karl M. Herrligkoffer published a record of the Everest expedition in a book.

what they mean. That may be a sufficient way into the arms of the church, but it isn't the way to God. Nature, which I love, is my preferred church. There's no incense on the peaks, nor do the bells ring, but that's where I really sense the presence of God.

'There were two facts about our Everest climb that proved significant: I was the first Pole on the summit, and I reached it on the day that Karol Wojtyla was elected Pope. Together they made me widely known in Poland and smoothed the way when I came to

The Japanese climber Junko Tabei (right) was the first woman to reach the summit of Everest, followed by the Tibetan Phantong (centre) and Wanda.

Wanda reached the top of Everest on the very day Karol Wojtyla was elected Pope.

Wanda and K. Chojnowska-Liskiewicz (with Minister Emila Wojtaszka) honoured in Warsaw in 1978 for sporting achievements which enhanced Poland's sporting reputation in the world

organize expeditions in later years. Every Pole could respond, because we all carry some kind of Everest of ambition in our hearts. Our Everests are all very different, and some are more spectacular than others, but none is less important. People saw my success as a kind of guarantee that we can all achieve whatever are our true ambitions.'

Cardinal Wojtyla's elevation to the papacy on 16 October 1978 as Pope John Paul II and his subsequent visit to Poland in July 1979 marked a turning-point for the Polish people, leading them from uncertainty to a rediscovery of strength in solidarity. During the

Pope's visit, Wanda was able to present him with a piece of Everest set in silver. 'I wasn't trying to boost either myself or my success. I just wanted him to know how deeply the coincidence of the two events had moved me. The Pope said, "It must have been God's will that we should both be set so high on one and the same day."'

'The idea that you can escape from ordinary problems in the mountains is a fallacy. You encounter every variety of the good and the bad, just as you do in the world below; though I must say that there's not much opportunity on the heights for intrigue, or what I call "the life behind my back". Of course, there's aggression in any group, and it escalates when you venture into the realms of the extreme. I think that facing up to difficulties makes me strong, whereas I am at my weakest when things run smoothly. Life is no easier down here. There may be less direct confrontation, and the spite and the meannesses may mostly pass you by, but it all comes out in the end and hurts you just as much.'

Wanda was for ever searching for people who would offer her understanding, but the response of the top Polish climbers to her success was jealousy.

Since her separation she had moved five or six times before finally she found a satisfactory apartment. Although she had been living there for two years, she still had found neither the money nor the time to furnish and equip it properly. 'It was a miserable background for the interviews and the photographic sessions that had become almost daily events. Journalists would arrive expecting to meet some happy summiteer. Instead they'd find a young woman who seemed to be incapable of dealing with her problems, or organizing her time, or even sorting the papers and the photographs that were strewn around every room. I was spinning into a real crisis, with panic attacks and a feeling that my world was collapsing.

'The more I had to tell the same stories again and again, the more alien they sounded, as though they had nothing to do with me at all. I felt as though I were reading some script written for someone else and totally irrelevant to any future "me". After Everest I wanted nothing more to do with expeditions or climbing. In fact I stopped climbing, though I never explicitly decided whether this was to be permanent or only a temporary break.'

Then in 1979 Maurice Herzog, the first man to conquer any 8000-metre peak when he scaled Annapurna, invited Wanda – together with the Japanese climber Junko Tabei and the Tibetan Phantong – to Chamonix to feature in a film he was making about women climbers in the Himalayas.

The trip offered Wanda the chance to climb once more on Mont Blanc, and she could not resist it. She teamed up with Irena Kesa and together they successfully climbed the Bonatti route on the east wall of the Grand Capucin and the 'American route' on the west face of the Petit Dru.

Wanda was paid $500 for her part in Herzog's film, and she used it to realize a long-held dream: to buy a second car for everyday use, an old Fiat 128. 'I'd qualified for a rally licence, and now I could afford to fit out my Polonez for competition driving.'

During this time she was working on the development of computer systems at the Warsaw Research Institute, where she was the first staff member to join Solidarnosc. 'Also, I'd gone back to climbing, though I'd not made any decisions about continuing my climbing career. The fact is that we Poles were dealing with altogether more important problems at the time.'

In 1981 there were probably about 5000 climbers among Poland's population of 36 million. They were regarded as slightly crazy freaks, addicted to unnecessary risk-taking, but when Polish expeditions began to record successes and Wanda conquered Everest there was a surge of interest, and an important economic by-product. For a while successful

After the Everest expedition Wanda was to discover that intrigue is as rampant off the mountain as on it.

climbers featured large in the media, and ranked in popularity with footballers and Olympic medallists.

In this favourable atmosphere Wanda was able to get approval – and Pakistani agreement – for a women's expedition to K2. At the end of February 1981 she set off with a few friends to do some winter training in the Caucasus. They managed an ascent of Elbrus without problems though the weather was terrible. But on the descent (on crampons), while Wanda was a little ahead of the rest of the group and therefore unaware of what was going on above her, some of the group got into difficulties. 'Suddenly I took a violent blow in the back. One of the other climbers had slipped and fallen straight down on top of me. I was completely unprepared and, try as I might to stop us with my ice-axe, we fell, rolling over and over. We were sliding faster and faster on sheer ice, and there was no way we could break our fall. The sling tore off my ice-axe and somewhere on the way down my leg struck a rock. When we finally came to a

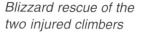

halt we had fallen 200 metres, and I realized that my leg was broken.'

While her companions were bringing Wanda off the mountain, they gave her alcohol to ease the pain. Later, in the ambulance, she vomited and behaved so strangely that there was, briefly, fear that she might have sustained a head injury. 'Then they attached two metal clamps to my femur and put a plaster on to my thigh. I could feel a movement in the bone right away which certainly shouldn't have been possible, but the doctors wouldn't believe me.'

When the Polish government introduced martial law on the night of 12/13 December 1981, after 18 months of an ill-tempered coalition between the Communist Party and Solidarnosc, Wanda was on a lecture tour in the East German GDR. On her return she was to undergo another operation to remove the metal clamps from her femur, but that was cancelled because of the confusion surrounding the State of Emergency. 'Immediately, I remembered my friendship of sixteen years earlier with Dr Helmut Scharfetter in Innsbruck, so I phoned him and asked him if he would be willing to operate on me.' It took a little while longer to jump through all the bureaucratic hoops required to be allowed to travel to Austria.

'It was an emotional meeting, as though those sixteen years had never intervened.

And why not? I thought. Better this marvellous man than the tanks on the streets at home. And anyway, I couldn't see anything wrong in needing Helmut and feeling dependent on him. It wouldn't be for very long, as I would soon be back on two legs, so why not just enjoy the feeling?' They married a few months after her operation, so Wanda was now Wanda Scharfetter and an Austrian citizen. Nevertheless she never used her new name except in official papers, preferring to stick with Rutkiewicz, which she had by then invested with her own sense of identity.

Helmut had divorced his first wife some years earlier, was living at Patsch near Innsbruck with his two sons, aged eleven and 12, and, fortunately, did not expect Wanda to become his cook and housemaid.

'Helmut lived among the beauties of the Tirolean mountain landscape, and his house was full of plants and animals. He started to educate me about the technological development trap by which our material civilization is poisoning our environment. These concerns were being discussed in the West long before they touched the public in Poland, and my talks with Helmut quite changed my way of thinking. The men and women who had developed the nuclear reactor had been my heroes but now I began to doubt whether reactors could make the world a better place.'

Helmut was a committed professional and he assumed that Wanda would also be pursuing her career, but unfortunately her leg had not properly healed and it fractured again when the metal clamps were removed. She needed crutches to walk, and was not allowed to put any weight on her damaged leg until the healing process was complete. 'Just standing up was sometimes unbearably painful, so it was pointless even to wonder whether I would ever climb again. And yet my stay in Austria gave me the gift of new experiences and the leisure to take objective

Snow-covered summit of Elbrus in the Caucasus

stock of myself. I believe that I grew during those weeks, thanks in no small measure to Helmut's influence.'

Wanda in hospital in the Soviet Union

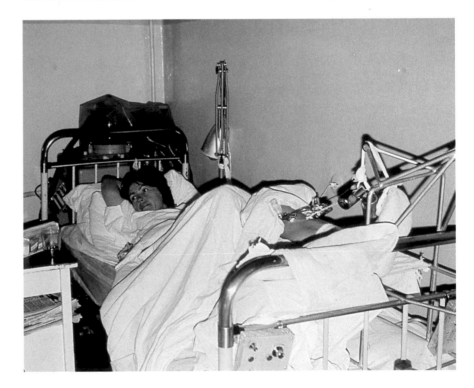

51

Hobbling to K2

The Himalayan 'Golden Age' had not yet ended when Wanda's first expeditions set forth. Like many other Polish climbers she was a beneficiary of certain aspects of the Communist system. When martial law was declared in Poland, the Pakistani expedition fee had, fortunately, already been paid, and the organization of the whole venture was so far advanced that the members unanimously decided to persevere. There was no foretelling how things might turn out in Poland, but there was a general and powerful will to hold on to a semblance of the normality for which the whole nation so much yearned.

In these circumstances Wanda decided that there could be only one realistic source of funds for her Polish women's K2 expedition: sponsors in the West. 'From where I was in Innsbruck this looked perfectly possible, and I pressed ahead with preparations in spite of my injury.' She faced two kinds of difficulty. First, it was difficult to keep in proper contact with her Polish colleagues, and secondly it was imperative to assemble funds and equipment. 'I was incredibly lucky to win the support of Reinhold Messner. I was especial-

---

The most recent surveys measure K2 at 8616m, which makes it the world's second-highest mountain. It has a multitude of names in many different languages – among them Balti, Urdu, Burushaski and Hindi: Chogori ('The Great Mountain'); Lamba Pahar ('Highest of All'), Dapsang ('Mighty Rock'), Lanfafahad, Kechu Kangri and Mount Godwin-Austen. However, the most current is the rather less romantic K2, wished on the mountain by the surveyor Montgomery who first located it in 1856 but could not discover what the locals called it. K2 is generally considered the toughest of the 8000-metre peaks, not least because the final summit stage involves some highly dangerous passages that have to be negotiated unroped.

In 1861 another Briton, H.H. Godwin Austen, began a survey of the Baltoro glacier, which grew into the first map of the region at 1:500,000. In 1902 an international expedition led by Oskar Eckenstein marched for four months to reach the foot of the mountain and attempt an ascent up the north-east spur, but at 6200 metres they declared the mountain to be unclimbable.

In 1909 an Italian expedition led by Luigi Amedeo of Savoy, Duke of the Abruzzi, rightly gauged that the southeast spur (since known as the Abruzzi Ridge) offered the best route, but were defeated at 6000 metres.

In 1938 an American expedition led by Charles Houston unlocked all the key pitches to an altitude of 7925m and one of the members, William House, succeeded in climbing a particularly difficult chimney (now named the House Chimney). However, Houston and Petzold had to give up within reach of success because they were not able to melt snow to drink, having forgotten to bring any matches from a lower camp.

In 1939 a German–American expedition led by Fritz Wiessner, climbing without oxygen, reached 8400m. Three Sherpas and Dudley Wolfe died when the upper camps on which their descent depended were taken down after a high-camp porter wrongly reported that the summit group had been killed in a fall.

In 1953 Charles Houston led another American expedition. This time one of the climbers, Art Gilkey, was taken seriously ill. In the process of trying to lower him a group of five climbers fell, but were held and secured by Pete Schoening. But as the team were pitching a new camp to continue the rescue, an avalanche swept Art Gilkey off the mountain.

In 1954 an Italian expedition mounted by Professor Ardito Desio got off to a bad start when Mario Puchoz died of a pulmonary œdema after two days in Camp III because no other team members were willing to delay their climb to carry him back to base camp. Later Walter Bonatti and a porter, Mahdi, also nearly died carrying oxygen bottles up the mountain to the summit party. Their target camp had not been set up exactly at the agreed point and they missed it in the darkness and high winds. The two men were forced to spend the night standing on a ledge on the rock face. Mahdi had been the man who carried Hermann Buhl down from Nanga Parbat with terrible frost-bite. Now he was himself severely frost-bitten. The team were rewarded on 31 August 1954, when Achille Compagnoni and Lino Lacedelli completed the ascent of the Abruzzi Ridge and became the first men to stand on the summit of K2.

In 1977 a huge Japanese expedition of 42 climbers and 1500 porters mounted a massive assault on K2, during which six climbers and a Hunza porter made the summit via the Abruzzi Ridge.

In 1978 three American climbers, John Roskelley, Rick Ridgeway and Lou Reichardt, made the first successful ascent without oxygen, and they were followed a year later by Reinhold Messner and Michl Dacher.

In 1986 Wanda Rutkiewicz was the first woman and the first Pole to reach the summit.

Wanda on the trail to base camp

ly grateful for his help because I was aware how often he had been exploited in the past, and even attacked by climbers whom he had helped in all sorts of ways. He was most sympathetic, even inviting me to accompany him on a lecture tour. I expect he felt sorry for me because I looked so helpless at the time.'

Reinhold Messner specially tailored some of the arrangements for his tour through northern Italy and down to Rome so as to allow Wanda to meet possible sponsors. Every one of his lectures drew an audience of a thousand or more and in every interval he made a point of introducing Wanda and enumerating her successes.

'My worst problem was getting on to and off stages without crutches. The pain was so bad that I'd be clenching my teeth, but of course I couldn't let it show.' Messner's

efforts succeeded in convincing sponsors that it might be worth supporting this crazed woman climber, crutches and all. Wanda was beginning to achieve some popularity in the West, and Italian and Austrian firms began to offer the latest in light-weight equipment, and money. 'The total was enough to fund the expedition on a scale I had never encountered on Polish ventures, and indeed it seemed there might even be money left over to put towards a future expedition. Our food supplies came from Poland and from some Austrian sponsors, while other Austrian companies supplied us with all our medical and pharmaceutical needs.'

The Polish Alpine Association took overall charge of the expedition, the Polish Sports Ministry paid the women's air fares, and there were some extra subsidies from the

French Ministry for Women's Rights. A Polish camera crew was added, to record the women's venture on film.

Wanda decided to join the expedition herself, pointing out that she had managed to climb in Poland notwithstanding her crutches and her plaster-cast. Her plan was to march the 150km up to base camp on those same crutches. 'Most people thought that was irresponsible of me, as the bones in my leg had still not properly fused.' But she was sure that she would be making the trek down without crutches after the weeks she would spend sitting at base camp.

'It was a challenge, to do something that most people were saying was impossible, but I wanted to be there because I felt responsible for my expedition. Anyway, I liked the idea of a challenge that most people said was senseless, indeed impossible, for anyone with a disability.'

Each of the twelve top climbers chosen already had extreme routes to their name, climbed in women-only ropes or had been members of major expeditions. Some of them had been on Gasherbrum II (8035m) or

Gasherbrum III (7952m) in 1975.

The complete list was:

Alicja Bednarz from Krakow, 45, secretary, 20 years' experience;

Anna Czerwinska from Warsaw, 32, doctorate in pharmacy, 12 years' experience, one of the women winter climbers of the North Face of the Matterhorn;

Halina Krüger-Syrokomska from Warsaw, 43, married with a 10-year-old daughter, journalist and children's-book editor at a Warsaw publisher's, 25 years' experience mainly in all-women ropes, Wanda's partner on Trollryggen and member of the Gasherbrum expedition;

Aniela Lukaszewska from Katowice, 32, married with a child, physicist, 10 years' experience;

Jolanta Maciuch from Warsaw, the expedition's medical officer, 29, 9 years' experience;

Anna Okopinska from Warsaw, 33, physicist, 15 years' experience, member of the Gasherbrum expedition;

Krystyna Palmowska from Warsaw, 32, doctorate in electronics, 12 years' experi-

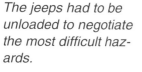

The jeeps had to be unloaded to negotiate the most difficult hazards.

ence, another of the women winter climbers of the North Face of the Matterhorn;

Ewa Pankiewicz from Lodz, 30, chemist, married with one child, 12 years' experience;

Danuta Wach from Katowice, business woman, married with one child, 15 years' experience, Wanda's partner on the second ascent of the north buttress of the Eiger;

Marianna Stolarek from Wroclaw; and finally

Christine de Colombel from Paris, who had first suggested the expedition, 35, journalist, top climber of extreme routes such as the Walker buttress on Mont Blanc's Grandes Jorasses, member of expeditions to Alaska, Peru and the Karakorum, almost reached the summit of Masherbrum in 1980.

By 30 June the whole team had arrived in Pakistan. 'We never sensed any ill-will or intolerance because we were women, only hospitality and respect. Naturally, we were warned not to infringe religious or national customs. We arrived during Ramadan, so we were advised not to eat in public places and not drink or smoke. We realized that we must always be acceptably dressed, notwithstanding the heat (45°C in the shade). We were often invited into people's homes and thus had the chance to observe family life at first hand.'

The entire baggage of the expedition was carried from Delhi in India to Islamabad in Pakistan and on to Skardu in Baltistan by truck. There were problems with permits and public authorities, as there always are, but some friendly support from the Pakistani climber Nazir Sabir, who had set up his own company 'Karakorum Tours', helped to smooth the way, until finally the Polish women could move on to Skardu, the capital of Baltistan.

Skardu is an extended desert settlement of some 10,000 inhabitants, set above the Indus which, at this point, winds like a gigantic snake through a flat area of sand dunes. Patches of vegetation and trees are few and far between; there seems to be no such colour

as green. The ancient trading post is ringed by barren yellowish-brown hills. Fierce-looking Baltis in baggy trousers stroll through the dusty alleys of the bazaar among the traders calling their wares. The few women to be seen scamper away and hide as soon as they see strangers. They are their husbands' property and they must not allow any strange man to look at them.

On 7 July three jeeps and seven tractors transported the expedition up the last stretch of rough track to the road-head at Dassu in the lunar landscape of the Braldo valley. The valley, above and beside the river, is rarely touched by the monsoon and remains almost permanently dry and arid. The torrential brown, muddy waters of the Braldo river hurl boulders, rubble and sand down to the lowlands. The Baltis of the valley are farmers: wherever tributaries from the barren slopes flow into the Braldo they have constructed complex, precisely-regulated irrigation systems to create little oases where patches of lush green break the grey monotony of the parched landscape. Grey rock outcrops, yellow sand and white rubble alternate with terraced fields edged with apricot trees. The precious earth is held by cleverly-constructed walls. Each family grows what it needs in these fields, and the apricots are dried on the roofs of their mud huts.

The bridges over mountain torrents can be precarious.

The Romantic poets' favourite flower

The convoy finally reached the road-head after a long drive in extreme heat through torrents, across flimsy suspension bridges and over other improbable structures supposedly designed to resist the flood waters. 'We pitched camp in Dassu and hired 260 porters for several days to carry our equipment up to our base camp.' That evening an atmosphere of satisfaction reigned among the tents. Blue smoke rose from the village houses as darkness fell gently on the valley while the peaks still shone in the last warm light of the day.

Every expedition depends heavily on its porters. If porters did not exist there would have been fewer expeditions and quite a number of the world's 8000-metre peaks would probably still be unscaled. Climbers and adventure-seekers would soon have tired of carrying their own heavy loads, which might have been a blessing for the Himalayas. Until quite recently the few expeditions that penetrated into Baltistan provided some welcome income to those men who had no fields to work and could afford to be away from home for months at a time. But today the region is overrun by expeditions and porters in search of engagements, for which they sign on by appending a thumb-print to their contracts. The quicker they can deliver their load, return home and be available for the next job, the more they earn. Their pay for one expedition is said to be about the equivalent of the value of one year's work on the land, and the strongest young men, who can manage several marches every season, can earn more in a year than the officers who accompany the expeditions.

Not all the effects are good, however. Not so long ago the people of Baltoro could be self-sufficient and live by barter. But today they depend on the expeditions, neglect their agriculture, have to buy in most of their food, and clothe themselves in expedition cast-offs. For the moment this is a flourishing economic system, but if it were interrupted, the effect on the porters and their families would be catastrophic.

The track to base camp runs along the Braldo river as it rushes down from its source in the Baltoro glacier. 'We left civilization behind as we took our first steps from the road-head and it receded by the hour. It was with mixed feelings that we passed through the last mountain villages over the next three days.' Even by the standards of this mountain terrain, life here was exceptionally harsh. Many of the men and women suffer from physical or mental abnormalities, many caused by iodine deficiency and in-breeding. Wives command high prices, often only affordable by first-born men, and a wife from another village will cost five times as much as one from a man's own village. Because the men spend long periods away from home, three or four brothers will often marry the same wife, so as to make life simpler and save money. Nor does this seem to provoke family jealousies.

'Our porters' care for one another, and their pride when they showed us their children filled me with admiration.' The children's hair is matted, their dirty faces sticky, their feet unshod (though with soles as tough as leather) and their little bodies clothed only in rags. No one makes them wash or go to school, or tells them what they may or may

Women and children working the fields of Askole

not do. When they grow strong enough, they begin to help their parents at work. No Balti child has ever slept in a bed. An earth floor and a few blankets serve instead, and when the icy mountain wind blows in through every crack, adults, children and animals all huddle together for mutual warmth. These children have little today and have no future. It takes only the slightest illness to snuff out their lives.

By 10 in the morning the sun reaches the last patch of shadow in the valley, and soon the land is throbbing like an oven in the intense heat. Sometimes the track is clear, but often it disappears, or divides into smaller tracks and little dead ends, with little indication of where the way should lie. But the porters know, even though the path is constantly moving, as the water-level of the Braldo

changes. The moraine slopes become steeper and more unstable on either side, and the track now runs through a narrow gorge where the roar of the river drowns the sound of the continual life-threatening rock-falls.

For Wanda, as she hobbled up this rough terrain on her crutches, hour after hour and day after day, the road to her dreams seemed to stretch away to infinity.

At last the valley opens again and the worst of the danger is over, but there is no easing of the track. Unstable under foot, it zig-zags up and down the valley sides, not gaining much height overall but very effectively exhausting the body. For the weary trekkers it is like walking in the concentrated beam of a magnifying glass: not a tree to be seen, nor the tiniest bit of shade. There is a wind, but so far from refreshing the body, it only gums up the eyes and covers the terrain

The oases of green in the stony wilderness of the Braldo valley are the product of a sophisticated irrigation system.

57

and everything on it that moves in a layer of grey-brown sand and dust. Look up, and even the blue sky is veiled in grey.

Yet even in this harsh valley there are humans eking out a meagre existence. Every now and again a few patches of green unexpectedly appear like some mirage: a few huts, the cries of children, weather-beaten faces looking up from the fields. Children crouch on the ground in semi-circles, shouting, whispering, hiding from the strangers, only to peek out again from behind walls and return to their noisy games.

Six-and-a-half hours later the weary marchers reached another village, where gradually all the climbers and the porters assembled and set to organizing a camp for the night. As they worked, more and more inquisitive villagers swarmed around them until it was hard to distinguish them from the porters. Now an additional imperative was to guard the equipment from mysteriously disappearing.

The women sat down to their supper in great contentment. They were by now on excellent terms and this strange world had cast a potent spell over them. Here was an alternative life and a very different one from their existence at home. Weeks of sleeping on the ground; no electricity; but their minds had discovered a new realm in which any yearning for modern comforts seemed out of place.

A little below Askole, the last village along the track, there is a pool formed by a hot sulphur spring. 'The porters were not keen to sit themselves down in the "stinking" water, but we were not going to miss the chance of a bath. We were so encrusted in a hard paste of dust and sun cream, and our hair so matted and full of grit, that it took time and effort to get clean. The best treatment for our hair would have been a steel curry-comb.' It had been days since they had been able to wash properly. Where there had been water there had always been other people, and no one has yet invented a way to

wash fully dressed.

'We had got to know the village chief of Askole, Haji Madhi, in 1975, and he now sold us seven goats to feed our porters, and made us a gift of an eighth as a token of friendship. By next morning the goats were looking really thin. Haji had fed them large quantities of salt so that they would drink enough water to make them look fatter than they really were. What can you say about a mind like that?'

The cold roused the Baltis long before first light, and the rattling of pots and the sounds of the waking village soon woke the last sleepers. The stars faded into a dull grey sky, lightening as the first rays of the sun illuminated the craggy peaks. The morning air was sharp enough to get everyone going, and the whole caravan was soon on the move again.

Above Askole the colour of the waters of the Braldo ran gradually paler, almost milky-white, as the marchers entered the magnificent, untamed approaches to the Baltoro glacier. Crossing the mighty glacier means finding a safe route through the ever-shifting grit-covered ice dunes and the huge crevasses. It was hard for Wanda to stay close enough to her group to keep them in sight, so she sometimes joined one of the little groups of porters who would stop every now and again to put down their packs and rest their backs. But then they would sprint off again, and their stop–start rhythm was killing for a European.

The next few days were full of dangerous little rock pitches and perilous river crossings where any false step could spell disaster, and the unbearable heat drained the women's strength. But the porters, even with their huge loads, seemed to glide serenely over every obstacle.

In the course of the day little rivulets swelled into fierce torrents and fording the rushing glacier melt often meant taking off boots and rolling up trousers to ford, but on these occasions Wanda's crutches gave her

Haji Madhi. Wanted for sharp practice!

an advantage. The icy water numbs the feet in seconds, and because you cannot feel where you are stepping, you bruise and injure your toes on the stones. Once on the other side the circulation only re-establishes sensation after several minutes of excruciating pain. The porters join hands to help one another through the roaring streams and the relief shows on their faces each time they emerge safe and sound.

'No one ever had to wait for me or take special care of me. But two Polish men climbers who were marching to K2 on another expedition saw me hobbling and felt so sorry for me that, late in the day, Jerzy Kukuczka picked me up and carried me over the home stretch on his back, and Wojtek Kurtyka carried me over one particularly dangerous stream.'

There are quite a few spots on Baltoro that have names like villages even though no one lives there. One such is Paju, a little oasis on a steep rocky hillside, just large enough for a bit of terraced meadow, some shady trees and a few flowers beside a pellucid spring. In the surrounding waste land it is a miniature paradise, set on the very edge of the glacier itself. Beyond Paju the vast mass of ice, ridged like a stormy sea and surrounded by sheer granite cliffs, fills a 60km stretch of the valley.

The caravan halted at Paju to distribute the porters' provisions and redistribute loads. The porters enjoyed their rest day and slaughtered their goats – not a sight for sensitive souls. But the meat was soon grilling over fires, setting the juices running, and in no time nothing was left of the goats but a few bones. As evening fell the Baltis began to sing and clap and, when two of the men began to dance, the climbers stopped work and did their best to join in. As the flames of the fires died down, the glow of the embers tinted the camp red and an infinity of stars shone in the black sky. Huddled groups of porters sang far into the night, long after the women had crawled into their sleeping bags.

There is no track across the grit and the rubble on the Baltoro glacier. Because the humps and hollows of the ice are in perpetual motion, every expedition has to find its own, new route. Only occasionally is the monotonous grey of the moraine broken by a patch of visible, grey-green ice, or by huge boulders festooned with great pinnacles of ice, or deeply cleft by streams of water. Sometimes there are ways round these streams, but more often the marchers have to wade up to the hips through the icy water, giving one another a helping hand, for the bed of the stream is treacherous – slippery under foot, or non-existent where water drops down a hole to flow underground.

'As the days passed, my skills on my crutches would have been the pride of a circus artiste; and I do believe that I never did my bad leg any damage.'

Urdukas is a grassy terrace at 4000m, directly facing the Trango Towers. Urdukas's name, 'broken rock', refers to a gigantic boulder field at the edge of the glacier. The trail up the valley and over the 6000-metre Mustagh Pass between Pakistan and China has been a trade route for many centuries, and the old traders sheltered from the cold and the storms in the caves at Urdukas where

The viewing platform at Urdukas

The Trango Towers

The porters had to carry their heavy loads through countless ice-covered glacier streams.

now the women and the porters huddled together over their cooking fires. The damp wood crackled and glowed, but mainly produced clouds of dense smoke which threw ghostly shadows on the cave walls. The petrol cookers were more effective in fouling the caves with their pestilential smell than in cooking. The porters sat out the night in misery, their teeth chattering and their bodies shaking with the cold.

When the first grey light announced the coming day, the relief was universal. In the dull morning light, misty clouds shrouded the glacier, but above them rose the sheer, 2,000-metre crags of the Trango Towers, fantastical yet seemingly close enough to touch. Wanda's instinctive response was to start spying out routes up the ridges and buttresses. Given the chance, she would have made straight for the Towers. 'I'd love to know what those rocks feel like to the touch. From where we were, the Trango Towers looked like a mirage that might vanish at any moment. I'll return one day and climb them.'

The sun had yet to reach the glacier. The little pools and the ice swamps lay under a thin, treacherous covering of ice. The porters trudged stiffly and silently up the wide moraine, chilled to the bone by the icy cold.

They passed by the three great stone cairns that preserve the memory of the many Baltis who have died tragically in crevasses or from sheer cold on their march over Baltoro to the K2 base camp. When the gods summon another Balti, his friends set another stone on one of the cairns – which never cease to grow.

The porters kneeled and prayed for Allah's protection on the glacier, and on this day their prayers were noticeably longer and more intense than their usual ritual. Back on their feet they led the caravan safely through the labyrinth of boulders and ice pinnacles in which it seemed impossible to see far enough to keep a sense of direction. It took a whole day to cross the mighty confluence where the Baltoro glacier, the Godwin Austen and a number of other glaciers all meet.

As the caravan climbed, the scenery became yet more spectacular. The Mustagh Tower, 7236m, rises sheer out of the glacier; the rectangular form of the Chogolisa, 7654m, shines like silver; the summit of Mitre Peak is arched like a bent needle; the effect of Masherbrum, at 7821m and the steep pyramid of Masherbrum IV and Broad Peak, 8047m, exceeds all fantasy. The mighty lord of Baltoro is the last to reveal himself: 3500 metres of sheer rock towering over the perpetual ice. 'K2 literally takes your breath away!'

As darkness fell, the porters made their camp for the night, digging stones out of the

ice to build low walls which they covered with sheets of plastic. These primitive shelters soon lay under a covering of white frost, and the porters cowered under them, too cold to sleep, coughing and singing quietly while the hours dragged by.

Next morning, after their usual prayers, the porters began their final day's march. Fresh snow had fallen, hiding the crevasses and making progress even harder. Every now and again a porter or a climber would sink ankle-deep or even waist-deep, but each time the individual was able to work free without help. Near the Broad Peak base camp there was a welcome safe stretch over moraine. But the final lap to the base camp at the very foot of K2 was across the most dangerously crevassed ice of the whole march – fraught with such risk that no climbers in the European Alps and in their right minds, faced with such terrain, would even contemplate approaching it unroped.

Their luck had held throughout the approach. On 19 July, after only 11 days of quick, safe trek – and without any of the commonly-encountered porters' strikes – the women had reached the Godwin–Austen glacier and set up their base camp on the moraine at about 5100 metres.

That year of 1982 four different expeditions were trying their luck on the world's second-highest mountain – generally reckoned also to be the world's most difficult. A Japanese expedition was climbing from the Chinese side and two other expeditions besides Wanda's were climbing from Pakistan. An Austrian expedition led by Hans Schell and Georg Bachler had been granted the first slot on the Pakistani side and Wanda's the second, and both had selected the south-east ridge (the Abruzzi Spur). The fourth, a Polish–Mexican expedition led by Janusz Kurczab, was attempting a first ascent from the Savoia glacier up the north-west ridge. No woman had yet reached the summit, perhaps for no better reason than that none had ever been offered a place in a

summit team.

Of the Austrian expedition, Wanda's group found only Alois Furtner and the Pakistani liaison officer at base camp. Georg Bachler, Werner Sucher and Walter Lösch were on their way in perfect weather to the summit of Broad Peak, which they reached on 23 July. By 27 July they were back, and all five Austrians had begun their climb of K2.

The women were climbing without porters and with as little reliance as possible on oxygen. In the teeth of the intense heat Anna Czerwinska and Krystyna Palmowska had set up Camp I at 6100m by 21 July, and with help from Christine de Colombel, Camp II at 6700m by 27 July. The other women shuttled to and fro, carrying loads between the different camps. Even Wanda, crutches and all, managed the ascent across the glacier and through the ice fall to their advanced base camp at 5400m.

On 30 July, around midday, Anna Okopinska and Halina Krüger-Syrokomska arrived with loads at Camp II to find the Austrians there also, on their way to the summit. At 13.30 Halina radioed to base camp: she was in good humour and gave an amusing

account of their climb. Wanda asked her what she thought the next day's weather would bring, to which she answered: 'I'll just have to ask God what he's got in mind.' The weather had been perfect for some time – every expedition's dream.

After Halina signed off, the two women brewed up and then lay chatting in their tent. Suddenly Halina lost consciousness. For the next hour Anna and the Austrians, following radioed instructions from their medical officer, fought desperately to save Halina's life. They tried mouth-to-mouth resuscitation, heart massage and oxygen, but Halina was dead and nothing could revive her.

Halina and Anna had climbed Gasherbrum II, 8035m, without oxygen seven years earlier and stood on the summit together. They had climbed together in the Caucasus and the Alps, and both been members of the Makalu expedition. Halina had had 25 years' climbing experience …

'We couldn't begin to understand why Halina had died. Her death was, and remains, a mystery.' The various doctors on the mountain had a number of theories: a cerebral haemorrhage; a severe heart attack; a tumour on the pulmonary artery. Whatever the cause, it might equally have struck at home, though not fatally if surgery could have been immediate, but had been exacerbated by altitude. On the mountain there could be no helping her.

Halina's death determined every aspect of the expedition from then on. 'We felt numb, but we were unanimous that our dead companion could not be left to lie up on the mountain, to be stepped over by future climbers, picked at and finally devoured by the birds. They said that I must make the decision.'

The members of the K2 expedition (from left to right): Marianna Stolarek, Danuta Wach, Anna Czerwinska, Krystyna Palmowska (half-hidden), Jolanta Maciuch, Ewa Pankiewicz, Aniela Lukaszewska, Christine de Colombel, Anna Okopinska and Wanda

I knew what was in the mind of the group. Halina must rest in a proper grave, somewhere not accessible only to mountaineers. After all, her daughter might one day want to see it. 'We knew that we must bring her down from the 6700m camp, however difficult and dangerous the route.'

The other expeditions on the mountain were generous with help. The Austrians delayed their ascent to carry her body down the steepest pitches between the two high camps – the most difficult and the most dangerous part of the whole operation. It deserves to be recorded that these brave men risked their own lives in perilous avalanche terrain for a dead comrade. They were not alone: the Polish–Mexican expedition trudged for eight hours to add their help with the task of carrying Halina down. So, finally, Halina could be laid to rest by the Gilkey Rock, among whose cracks and clefts so many victims of K2 are buried or memorialized alongside the ever-creeping glacier.

'We said our farewells to Halina on 1 August, deeply moved by our community with all those other climbers who had reached out their hands and put aside their own ambitions to help us. Our gratitude for their concern and their efforts knew no bounds.' Indeed the Austrian expedition decided to attempt no further summit ascents, even though they would still have had time to try. Georg Bachler had an explanation: 'We were totally exhausted – not so much in body as in spirit – and we decided that another summit simply wouldn't be worth the effort.'

'We all felt the pain of Halina's absence in the days that followed. It was hard to believe that she had left us for ever. We all knew the risks and dangers on the mountains, and especially on extreme expeditions, but we had never pictured death on the mountain like this. In fact we had never truly imagined it at all because none of us had ever stood directly at its shoulder.'

Now the question was whether to continue without Halina. Poland was under martial law and life there was far from simple. None of the Polish women knew what would face her back home, so there was no obvious incentive to break off so soon. K2 was looking friendly in the sunshine and they were all free and independent agents. 'Would it be disrespect to Halina if we climbed on? Would she have wanted us to abandon our expedition for her sake?'

Time to start the day's climb

This was not an easy decision, and Wanda gave her colleagues time to agree on the right course of action. 'It began to emerge that we wanted to go on. Halina's close friend Anna Okopinska was the last to decide but she, like the rest of us, felt that Halina could survive among us in spirit a little longer in the mountains, whereas her memory would soon be submerged in the trivialities of our daily lives at home.'

On 7 August Colombel, Czerwinska and Palmowska made a reconnaissance climb to

Camp at the foot of K2

Climbing the aluminium ladders up the House Chimney

weather had been concentrated in the first three weeks.

On 16 September they finally gave up and brought all their equipment down from the high-altitude camps. They were determined not to abandon their precious gear, even at the risk of frostbite in the icy gale. Temperatures had fallen below zero even in their base camp where, by now, deep snow had fallen, the tents were being battered by the winds and sleep had become almost impossible. The porters were supposed to arrive on 23 September to transport the expedition back to the road-head, but the deep snow held them up for another three days.

'Our Baltis were every bit as dependable on the descent as they had been on the approach. If I had needed help over the treacherously snow-covered glacier, I'm sure they would have offered it. As it was, I regard the 150km of my marches up and down, through difficult terrain and on crutches, as one my most notable achievements. I doubt if anyone had ever got 5400 metres up a glac-

7100 metres, but almost immediately afterwards the weather began to deteriorate and, with it, the likelihood of any chance to go for the summit. Although there were periods of bright sunshine down at base camp, the summit of K2 was almost perpetually lost in cloud and the snow was blowing off its great ridges in vertical spin-drifts.

The women were not yet ready to give up, but conditions above 7000 metres were becoming intolerable. To attempt the summit, it would be imperative to establish a third high-altitude camp above the steep pitches of the Black Pyramid. They tried and tried, but the force of the storm was now well-nigh annihilating even at the lower level of Camp II.

Palmowska and Czerwinska scaled the Pyramid no fewer than six times. The other women fought to keep the existing camps in repair, against the depredations of wind and rock-fall, and volunteered to take their turn on the rock. They managed to get all the equipment they would need up to the new camp sites but, each time, they had to withdraw again, cruelly defeated in all their efforts to establish Camps III and IV. A few more days of the earlier good weather was all they would have needed. In all they were on the mountain for 69 days, but all the good

confirmed her view that the second – 15 June – slot was too late in the season for any ascent of the Karakorum from the south. Only the Japanese expedition had been successful, and they had climbed from China in the north, putting up the first ascent of K2's north buttress.

'Unlike our earlier venture on Gasherbrum III, this women's expedition had needed no outside expert leadership because we were all experienced alpinists ourselves.' Each of the climbers knew what was required of her. Moreover, their shared adventures and hardships had created strong bonds of friendship and mutual trust between them. Though the expedition had not achieved its ultimate aim it had laid strong foundations for future ventures. 'Knowing what we now knew, we determined to return to K2 one day and try our luck again, but a month earlier in the season. The world's most beautiful mountain had mocked our dreams and ambitions. We would have to come back and settle our account.'

ier against a handicap like mine. Mind you, I would perhaps have done better to stay at home, where my bone might have knitted and I'd certainly not have ended the summer in such poor condition.'

Wanda's expedition was that year's last on the Baltoro. Their failure to reach the summit

The women making full use of fine weather to establish their high-altitude camps

'The Mountain of Mountains' Second attempt

Wanda and three other Polish women climbers were back on K2 in the spring of 1984, with a commercial expedition of Germans, Austrians and British led by Stefan Wörner. Anna Czerwinska and Krystyna Palmowska, who had been with Wanda on K2 in 1982 and in the following year, climbing together as a women's rope, had climbed Broad Peak (8047m) without porters and without oxygen, though only Palmowska reached the summit, Czerwinska stopping a few metres below it. As a result the two women were now numbered among the international climbing élite.

The fourth member of the Polish team was Dobroslawa Miodowicz-Wolf, 31, ethnographer, married with a child, with 13 years' experience and a record including Pik Korshenevskaya (7105m), Pik Kommunismus (7483m), Krupska Peak in the Pamirs (c.6000m), extreme climbs in both summer and winter in the Tatra, Ullu Tau Tshana in the Caucasus, the 'Voie des Guides' on the Petit Dru, the 'Philip/Flamm' on the northwest face of the Civetta, the 'Vinatzer' on the south face of the Marmolada and the 'Paul VI route' on the Tofana di Rozes.

The four women joined the commercial expedition as an independent unit. Since they could not afford to pay Stefan Wörner the commercial fees, they had to bring their own equipment and food. Meanwhile the other members of the 1982 K2 team were climbing Meru Peak, a difficult 6000-metre summit in India's Garhwal Himal.

This time Wanda found the approach to base camp easy as never before. 'My leg had healed at last. I'd needed four operations over two-and-a-half years before I could walk my first few steps without crutches. And what a

happy moment that was!' Now that her leg was fully restored, Wanda seemed to have the strength of two. The expedition set up its base camp at the foot of K2 at 5100m after only 10 days' march.

A few more days were needed to ensure that everyone had acclimatized to the high altitude and that no members of the expedition were still suffering headaches or waking in the night struggling for breath.

The plan was to follow the classic ascent route up the Abruzzi Ridge. An advanced base camp was set up three hours' climb above the base camp to serve as a depot. It could also be used as an overnight stop: to allow an early morning climbing start; or a rest after climbing down the sheer ridge and before facing the dangers of the glacier on the way home to base camp. The perils on the stretch between the two camps are among the worst on the whole Abruzzi route. Huge avalanches hurl themselves onto the glacier with such force that they surge up the opposite slopes like breakers on a reef. New crevasses open and new torrents cut through the ice almost daily, so that yesterday's route may not be passable today.

However, this stretch offers the unique attraction of its seracs, those fantastical structures of shimmering ice, sometimes as much as 20 metres high, smooth as marble. They tower over the glacier like sculptures by forgotten giants – some gleaming in shades of blue and green, some glowing in milky-white opacity, some transparent like sparkling crystal. From time to time the heat of the sun and the extreme temperature swings bring one of these bastions crashing down. Between the seracs the surface of the glacier can become treacherous, especially in the late afternoon, when the semblance of firm snow may conceal sumps of icy slush which can swallow climbers to the knees, the hips or even the shoulders. Such dips are to be avoided even on the hottest of days. The descent to base camp is a long one, and wet clothes soon freeze into rigid suits of armour. A soaking may even cost a life.

Climbing upwards from the depot is exhausting, and a heavy rucksack soon dampens enthusiasm. At this altitude your heart thumps like a pneumatic drill, your lungs are at bursting point and the altitude saps all your reserves. The most difficult pitches on the face have some protection from fixed ropes left by previous expeditions, but they still need careful examination and repair. Progress along the fixed ropes, up rock and ice, up chimneys, climbing pitches and tracts of unstable material, is painfully slow. The fixed ropes are particularly welcome on pitches of Grade III and above, where rucksacks are an extra handicap and risk can be significantly decreased by clipping onto protection. In the rarified atmosphere the drain on physical strength is such that every limb is leaden.

The team set up Camp I at 6100m. This involved digging level platforms in the snow and ice for the tents, and fitting them out with foam mats, sleeping bags, cookers, gas containers and food. You can ignore the cold as long as you keep moving, but the nights are icy cold. To keep any warmth, you have no choice but to creep into your sleeping bag, and even that will be half full of your indoor footwear, your head lamp, cameras and radio, stored there to keep them from freezing. Cooking inside the tiny tents is a problem. Feeding a whole group of several climbers is a performance which can take hours.

Bad weather was holding the expedition back, as it had the previous one. K2 was rarely visible, wrapped in clouds, mists and wind spins. Occasionally the sun shone for a few hours and then the summit stood out above its wreath of cloud, glowing red in the afternoon light like a sinking fire. More often the outlook was dark and depressing, a mournful reflection of the ubiquitous perils of the mountain. The nights were loud with the sounds of danger: the thunder of avalanches and rock- and ice-falls; the menacing creaks and groans of the glacier. Their only safe place was base camp.

The climbers were restless, longing for progress, but the grey clouds rolled upwards from the glacier day after day, and the snow fell, sometimes for days on end. The Karakorum is noted for its bad weather, and even when conditions improve climbers must wait for at least the largest avalanches to fall. While the lower slopes are in shadow until midday the icy summit may be glistening in the sun like some fantastical icing-sugar creation. But the serenity of the panorama is an illusion: when the massive avalanches fall, the glacier trembles as though struck by earthquake. Snow rushes continuously down the south face like torrential water. The force of the great waves thundering onto the surface of the glacier drives them far up the facing slopes of Broad Peak, where they crest and break, to fall back on the glacier in huge balled masses.

However, the tents of Camp I were well protected from the avalanches under a rock overhang. Reaching the camp yet again, the women dug them out of the snow and set to work enlarging and improving the camp. Each climber understood exactly what to do and they worked in silence, knowing that every word was an unnecessary drain on their energy. Next morning, with their heavy rucksacks packed, they would attempt the next stage of the ascent. And indeed, after three hours of climb they had gasped their way to the narrow col at the foot of the House Chimney and established Camp II at 6600m. But the wind had changed, and storm clouds left no doubt that the weather was about to deteriorate again. The House Chimney was

Dobroslawa Miodowicz-Wolf, Anna Czerwinska, Krystyna Palmowska and Wanda (right to left)

shrouded in fog, so the women secured their camp and climbed down again. When humans challenge these giant mountains, all the experience and all the equipment in the world may count for nothing. The mountain will set the rules, and the rules may ignore the best-laid human plans.

Finally the weather took a longer turn for the better, and the women set out again with heavy loads of equipment and food to establish Camp III above the Black Pyramid. They were helped up the House Chimney by the steel rope ladders left by previous expeditions, still blowing in the wind. Above, the route was clearly marked by old fixed ropes leading to a steep ice slope directly below the Black Pyramid.

Their crampons scraped blue-black splinters of ice as they squealed and grated over the rock. Most of the fixed ropes proved to have deteriorated or been damaged by rock-falls and avalanches. The way to the next rock section lay up a 45° ice terrace where the fixed ropes had to be dug out of the snow or cut out of ice with their ice-axes.

Wanda was climbing like an unstoppable machine, step by step, higher and higher, up rock pitches all the way to 7000 metres. At last the climbers were on snow once more

and now the icy air stabbed painfully into their lungs. Their pace slowed: eight paces – then a rest, propped on an ice-axe, with aching head feeling as though it had swollen into some giant balloon too heavy for the body to support. A motionless minute was all it took to dispel this terrible sensation and allow the heartbeat to return to normal, but after just a few more steps the fight for breath would be on again and the exhaustion would be creeping back into leaden limbs.

Another snow field to cross, another painful trail to tread, before a mass of ice towers barred the way, forcing them to climb and chimney up a steep ice face, to reach a broad shoulder under deep fresh snow. As they crept forward in search of a safe route, with great packets of snow sliding slowly down towards them from the slopes above, they had to zig-zag to and fro to avoid being swept away. Now they could manage no more than three paces between rests, but they battled on, stamping spraddle-legged through the loose snow, then gasping and leaning all their weight on their ice-axes. Their weariness from climbing and their heavy loads was compounded by the vital need to search out the safe route. The fixed ropes lay so deep in the snow that they had to lay new protection, which meant setting snow anchors and driving in ice screws – all blood-freezing labour at such an altitude.

At last the women found a little patch that was sheltered from the avalanches and hacked a platform out of the ice. Setting up a new camp at 7300m was hard work indeed but, after a sleepless night, they climbed on. The ridge became steeper, there were no more old fixed ropes, and there were treacherous crevasses. Finally, at 7400 metres, the weather defeated them. Suddenly and without warning swirls of snow began to blow around all the visible peaks and ridges and buttresses of the Karakorum.

The first squalls struck within minutes, blowing shimmering spirals of crystals off the ground. Razor-sharp slivers of ice slashed their faces as a yellowish veil covered the blue sky. The rumble and the howling of the storm waxed so titanic and blew so mercilessly cold that they knew they must turn about. When at last they reached the fixed ropes and clipped themselves on the immediate danger of being blown away was over, but there was nothing for it but to get off the ridge as quickly as possible and head for the safety of base camp.

'I was in marvellous shape and had acclimatized very well, but all to no purpose because of the terrible weather. I was happy all the same because my leg had well and truly healed.' The expedition as a whole had to wind up because some of its clients had only limited holiday time, and Pakistani regulations would not allow the Polish women to continue on their own. The 'Mountain of Mountains' had defeated them again.

'We Poles had time but no money, whereas the climbers from the West had plenty of money but no time. But ours were the greater losses because we had had to invest both relatively huge amounts of time and money to be allowed our places, whereas the Swiss members only needed to guarantee their own fitness. The organizers saw to everything else – which is their job on every commercial expedition – so that the clients could enjoy the expedition as an adventure holiday.' The clients had pay and holiday to cover their costs, but if they were to report back late for work, they risked losing their jobs.

On her way home from K2 Wanda made a hopeless attempt to scale Broad Peak in the one day left to her – and actually reached 7150 metres.

When she got home, Wanda separated from her second husband Dr Helmut Scharfetter, the Innsbruck doctor, after only three years of marriage.

'When you're in love, nothing else matters and you accept one another as you are, with all your virtues and faults. But when reality cut in, we realized that we were increasingly hurting one another rather than forgiving. I had genuinely believed that I would want to make space for my marriage and for motherhood in my life, but once I realized that family life was not my style and I could see that the script of our marriage had no real part written in for me, then I saw no alternative to separation.'

So in 1985 Wanda moved back to Warsaw, lecturing and writing articles about mountaineering, but continued to spend some time in Austria, staying with friends in Vienna. A book of her writings was published in Poland. She had also been producing and directing films since 1982, and had become the first woman to shoot film at 8000 metres.

Honours for the ascent of the south face of Aconcagua

Summit cross

Lake Horcones on the track to Aconcagua

In 1985 Wanda organized herself a working visit to South America to attempt the south face of Aconcagua (6959m) alpine style with the well-known Swiss Alpine guide and adventure-holiday organizer Stephan Schaffter. Her commercial job was to lead a group to the summit by the normal route.

The south face rises sheer almost 3000 metres. The manifold perils include ice pitches, rock barriers, seismic disturbances which increase the risk of avalanches, unheralded weather changes, extreme cold and the fear-some 'white winds of the Andes' which can blow up to 200km/h. Between them these hazards can transform this wall of rock into a death-trap with no possible escape. In the southern hemisphere, of course, south faces are the colder and the more dangerous, corresponding to our north faces.

Wanda and Stephan had reached around 5000 metres when an avalanche broke from the snow above them. Stephan was filming. Wanda found some good holds, pressed herself against the face and covered her head

with her rucksack. The two climbers managed to cling on while the avalanche crashed over them, and the further avalanches that followed missed them.

'I had to sit down and rest my shaking legs. There were plenty more potential avalanches up there, threatening us all around, and suddenly the weather turned on us. We were trapped on this great cliff.' But after they had sat out the weather for 24 hours, it improved again and they were able to complete their climb and stand on the summit – in the ultimate stages of exhaustion but buoyed by success. They lost no time in starting down the normal route. 'We were fighting for survival, literally crawling on all fours.' They left the summit at five in the afternoon and by nightfall they had reached the foot of the rock, 3000 metres below.

Wanda ranked this climb among her greatest achievements, and the Polish authorities marked her accomplishment by awarding her an honour at the 50th anniversary of the first Polish expedition to the Andes, which had climbed Aconcagua in 1935.

South face of Aconcagua from the summit ridge

Nanga Parbat

Terror on the summit

The two failed attempts on K2 had left Wanda with a dividend of a little money and a good deal of equipment, which in 1985 she decided to invest in a women's expedition to Nanga Parbat, where the approach to base camp was only three to four days' march, as against the eleven days of the trail to K2. Moreover, the cost of porterage would be a great deal less. Wanda chose three exceptional partners: Anna Czerwinska, Krystyna Palmowska and Dobroslawa Miodowicz-Wolf. The team of four had already been tried and tested on K2. 'Anna and Krystyna deserve special mention. We were never on the most intimate personal terms, but our relationships always seemed to work well.'

Nevertheless, the burdens of organizing the expedition made Wanda feel exploited, and she determined, as she worked, that she would never take on the organizer's task again. 'Maybe my partners were less committed because they regarded Nanga Parbat as a less prestigious peak than K2. The exception was Dobroslawa, who worked just as keenly as I did. When necessity calls, I can do the impossible, and I felt the others exploited that. I want partners to pull their weight for the common aim. I don't like working for other people if they take me for granted.'

The expedition went very much according to plan. The team lost little time in setting up their series of high-altitude camps on the Diamir face, in spite of some bad weather, but had to postpone their summit attempt when their highest camp was buried by an avalanche, forcing the women back to a lower camp. They planned to carry this camp higher up the mountain next day in order to mount the final assault from the most favourable possible start.

Dobroslawa, however, was unwilling to lose so much time and decided to stay at the site of the buried camp, bivouacking in the open alongside Peter Habeler and Michl Dacher, who had managed to find their cooker and a bit of food in the remains of the avalanche. The men set off early and reached the summit before the weather deteriorated. On their way down they met Dobroslawa, climbing slowly, and tried to persuade her to turn about, but she was unpersuadable and continued her trudge up into the mounting storm. Suddenly she thought she could see Jerzy Kukuczka and hear him talking to her. Now Jerzy was indeed on Nanga Parbat at the time, but on a quite different part of the mountain. When she thought, a little while later, that she saw a Pakistani woman in a chador she realized that she must be hallucinating.

Meanwhile the other three women had carried the lower camp up and, once they had reset it, stood out in the blizzard to try to ensure that Dobroslawa could not miss the camp. 'Suddenly I made out a dim ghostly figure, tossed in the wind, but heading straight for the camp.' Dobroslawa had been forced to retreat just below the summit, but she was safe.

Next morning Wanda helped Dobroslawa down to the top of the fixed ropes, while Anna and Krystyna, who were loath to lose another day, moved up from the camp towards the summit. When they failed to find the route to the summit ridge they returned to the top camp. The following day the three

Summit mass of Nanga Parbat from the west

women at last stood together on the summit. Krystyna and Anna were first, but Wanda joined them an hour later, to be photographed on the summit with a sponsor's emblem visibly attached to her ice-axe. 'We women had scaled the summit of Nanga Parbat by the Kinshofer route and without oxygen! But even as I stood there I began to feel electricity in the air. I could hear the discharges hissing around me and my ears hurt. I remembered the many stories of climbers who had been killed by lightning and I knew that we had to get off the mountain fast.'

Descending alongside the summit ridge rather than along the crest was no easy matter. Wanda's best refuge from the danger of lightning bolts was to go on all fours and keep her head below the level of the ridge.

'Not particularly heroic – but I was truly scared of being killed.' Krystyna and Anna were quicker down, but they waited for Wanda at the top of the snow couloir into the rock face which was the steepest and most dangerous section of their descent. Just before darkness fell the three women were at last back on level ground.

Wanda was not yet done with Pakistan for the year. She teamed up with Barbara Kozlowska from Poland and Stephan Schaffter for another attempt on Broad Peak (8047m). They decided on separate ascents, Stephan having opted to try for the summit in a single day, Barbara preferring to go over three days. There could be no doubting her skills as a climber, but she had had no experience of

73

High camp on Nanga Parbat

Wanda on the fixed ropes just below the highest camp

expedition climbing and soon had to turn back. The cwm at the foot of the mountain holds a glacier, and not far above base camp Barbara had to cross a glacier stream which, though almost dry when she had crossed in the morning, was now running thigh-deep over a bed of smooth ice that made the crossing highly dangerous even though it was protected by fixed ropes. Barbara had not put on

crampons: her legs were swept from under her by the current and she could not muster the strength to get back on her feet. She died of cold, still hanging on to the fixed rope.

Meanwhile the weather deteriorated, so that Wanda and Stephan also had to admit defeat at 7800 metres. 'It was a dreadful shock to find Barbara hanging in the water. We laid her body temporarily in an ice hollow in the moraine and covered it with rocks.' It was Wanda's intention to come back the following year with some companions to give her friend a proper burial.

An exceedingly unpleasant surprise awaited Wanda on her return to Poland. She found herself accused of embezzlement from the funds of her recent expeditions. In the Polish administrative system expeditions had to present detailed accounts of all their expenditure. Because, in the past, virtually every expedition had ended with a deficit, there had never been an accounting problem. But Wanda's K2 expedition, with its Western sponsors and Western equipment, had been left with a surplus, which she had re-invested in her two following expeditions. Some of the money had been stolen from her in Delhi, and the Polish scrutineers demanded that she repay the amount of the stolen money to the organizing committee. No matter that she had hobbled round the West on crutches to raise the money. By granting it to the Polish Mountaineering Fund she had, they maintained, forfeited all rights to the money but could still be held responsible for it. 'I had never been so unjustly treated in all my life …'

The officials tried to justify their action by claiming that previous expeditions, which had claimed to have lost or been robbed of money, had in fact lined their own pockets by buying illicit foreign currency. Wanda never accepted that she should have been singled out for suspicion and punishment and decided, then and there, never to organize another expedition from Poland.

K2

Light and shade

Organizing her own expeditions had proved an unhappy experience, and Wanda decided it would be better to buy her way onto others' expeditions with money earned by shooting films. 'My first two films – "Join me on these rocks" and "Aconcagua Tango" – were so well received that I decided to work on my skills as a film-maker.' When ÖRF (Austrian television) paid her a substantial advance for a film from K2, she used the money to buy a place on a French expedition. 'It meant I could make films instead of wasting my time on organization. Of course high-altitude filming is awkward and very hard work, but I was hoping that the connection with ÖRF could prove even more fruitful in the future.'

K2 is Pakistan's favourite mountaineering destination, and in 1986 the Pakistani authorities issued a record number of permits to no fewer than nine expeditions.

1 A Polish Karakorum expedition led by Janusz Majer were heading for the 'Magic Line', which Reinhold Messner had had to abandon in 1979, but on which a French expedition had since then reached 8400 metres.

2 'Quota 8000' from Italy, including the Austrian Kurt Diemberger and the English-woman Julie Tullis, were attempting a new route on the south-west buttress.

3 An international K2 expedition led by Karl M. Herrligkoffer and including two Poles, Jerzy Kukuczka and Tadeusz Peotrowski, were attempting to scale the 3500 metres of the south-west face by the Sichel couloir.

4 A South Korean expedition was climbing the Abruzzi Ridge with Sherpas and oxygen.

5 The first-ever team of Austrian mountain guides was also climbing the Abruzzi Ridge, led by Alfred Imitzer.

6 The Italian Renato Casarotto was attempting a solo climb of the 'Magic Line'.

7 An American expedition made up a third group on the 'Magic Line'.

8 A British expedition was ascending by the west ridge.

9 The French–Polish expedition, consisting of Liliane and Maurice Barrard (whom Wanda had met on Broad Peak in 1985), Michel Parmentier and Wanda Rutkiewicz, were also aiming to reach the summit by the Abruzzi Ridge, but alpine style and in the shortest possible time.

Remembering the bad weather of 1982, Wanda made sure that this expedition should arrive at the very beginning of the season. Renato Casarotto, his wife and the expedition's medical officer arrived at base camp in

Liliane and Maurice Barrard, Wanda's partners on the K2 expedition

Wanda filming at base camp

Base camp

April, where they had to sit out several weeks of bad weather. When Wanda and her team arrived they set up Camp I at 6300m and a food and equipment store higher up, instead of a Camp II. Meanwhile a whole tented city was growing at base camp.

'It is most important for expeditions on the same territory to work together, help one another, never compete or do anything on the mountain that might disadvantage others. That year there were really too many expeditions on the Abruzzi Ridge, and most of them were not actually entitled to be there, having been driven off the more extreme routes by bad conditions. There were Pakistani officials on duty, but it's so difficult to tell a passionate mountaineer that you're not allowing him to attempt a climb.'

There was no way to punish these 'illegals' until the end of the season, when they could be put on to Pakistan's black list, thus incurring a hefty fine and a ban of several years from any mountain requiring permits.

'Maurice and Liliane were against lines of fixed high-altitude camps, preferring to carry light tents as part of their load and bivouacking wherever time and conditions dictated. Only a few years earlier climbers were still of the opinion that only madmen would venture onto the highest peaks without oxygen,

but we took none. The contrast between my first Everest expedition, with all its Sherpas and oxygen bottles, and this light-weight K2 venture couldn't have been greater. My self-imposed anti-fear training certainly came into its own …'

When Wanda and her companions set out for the summit, they were able to pick up supplies and equipment from the stores they had set up, and thus avoid spending nights in higher camps. 'This meant we got to the highest bivouac positions without all the exhaustion and risk involved in establishing full camps. It was Maurice's idea to experiment with this technique, and I was quick to agree because I was sure I could manage anything that he believed was within his wife's powers. The Barrards were an important influence on me, and I felt that they had the perfect marriage, equally happy in the mountains as in their daily groundling life. I have always found marriage a brake on my life, and I would never want to climb with a husband. The bonds of a marriage are not the same as the bonds between members of an expedition, and I need independence in the mountains. Within the community of an expedition, a couple is liable to constitute a sub-group who may provoke tensions. But the Barrards proved that this needn't always be the case.'

However, there were some problems when Wanda and Michel could not agree to share a tent. This meant that the common load had to include an extra tent, good camping spots might have to be ignored for lack of space for a third tent, and each of them had to dig out a separate tent platform instead of sharing and reducing the work. But Wanda found Michel's manner so unbearable that she preferred to carry the extra loads, even though she readily admitted that 'Michel more than pulled his weight in the laborious business of blazing the trail through the snow on the Abruzzi Ridge, which was still virgin because we were the first expedition to go. The rest of us could not match his stamina.

Up to about 7800 metres they had not needed to use their rope, depending on old fixed ropes or climbing free where those were broken. They avoided most of the rock pitches, preferring to climb on steep ice and snow slopes. To 7000 metres or so there is no call for skills beyond Grade IV. There is some unstable rock, but the fixed ropes offer good protection.

Michel was first to the bergschrund at about 7800 metres, but he punched a hole in the snow bridge as he crossed. When Liliane looked through it at the bottomless abyss below, she took fright and asked for the rope. But the rope was in Michel's rucksack, who had tramped on and refused to come back.

'It's no problem' was his only response as he marched on. The other three thought it was a sufficient problem to warrant searching for an alternative crossing. When they found it, it had involved a long detour, a climb, unroped, up a steep ice pitch, some help from Maurice, who was the tallest, for the two, smaller women, and the loss of two precious hours. Cold and angry, they were forced to spend an icy night at 7900 metres, four in a single tent without sleeping bags and with only the minimum of equipment required for their intended day-time summit ascent and descent.

The only more level section on the shoulder of K2 was under the deepest snow, and forcing a way through it cost them more energy and time than they had planned. They had now unanimously agreed to abandon the rope to save carrying its three-kilo weight, but the most difficult section of all – the ice-covered 'Bottleneck' – still lay ahead.

There were no fixed ropes here, so they could not risk the slightest fall. Perhaps in better conditions this section may have been less fearsome, but now the rock slabs were completely coated in a thin layer of ice,

High camp on the Abruzzi Ridge

77

Above 7000 metres, treading a route in deep snow is inconceivably exhausting work.

Wanda and her companions somehow put the 'Bottleneck' and the ice traverse behind them, but then found themselves in chest-high snow, with no choice but to spend a second night in the Death Zone.

The final stretch to the summit lay over a long shoulder which, in their state of exhaustion on that icy cold morning of 23 June 1986, seemed endless. Maurice, Liliane and Michel stopped to rest and brew up some tea, but Wanda was not keen to spend a moment longer than necessary at this altitude, and stomped on alone.

'Climbing on alone was really exciting, and I was thrilled to be so near the summit, etched ahead like a crown with three points. It was a beautiful day. My dream of reaching the second-highest peak in the world – so much more beautiful than Everest – was coming true and the weather couldn't have been more perfect for the occasion. When I stood alone on the very top it was 10.15. Around me lay a stupendous ring of slightly lower mountains. Clouds hung in the valleys below, and above was nothing but the infinite expanse of the sky.'

Wanda was the first Pole and the first woman to scale K2, and she stood there alone, savouring the taste of success. The wind blew fiercely but the air was clear.

'I've set myself a lot of tough targets at one time or another. I've survived a lot of adventures and had my highs and lows. Life hasn't always been smooth … But at that moment I felt I had a gift of infinite time. My friends were still a long way below. It was my name day, which in Poland is much more important than your birthday. I thought of my family, and I felt an infinite gratitude for the privilege of standing on this spot. I felt no triumph, but I did feel that God was near me. I've always felt close to God at the top of difficult mountains.'

Wanda wrote the date and time, her own name and that of Liliane Barrard on a piece of card, over the proud legend 'First

compacted and clear as glass, with absolutely no hand-holds or foot-holds. The only way to progress up the steep slope was by friction, applied by crampons below and pressure against an ice overhang above. Beyond the 'Bottleneck' they had to cross a long, exposed traverse of deep, hard ice with plunging views down on to the glacier below: another section in which to avoid errors. 'It would have been wonderful to find some fixed ropes up there, but who's going to drag ropes up to that sort of altitude? And anyway the rock and the ice were so hard that it would have been almost impossible to fix any kind of protection.'

women's ascent', wrapped the card in a little plastic bag and secured it under a stone just to the north of the main summit.

As the time passed, Wanda began to feel uneasy. Finally she could wait no longer and started down to meet the others. When at last they appeared she climbed back to the summit with them. 'Bursting with pride, Maurice said 'We're the highest couple in the world', and hugged Liliane, who was weeping with joy and said, 'It's the first time I've ever been on a summit in such perfect weather. I can see the whole world.' Then she exclaimed, 'But what's this? The other mountains are growing higher. We're not the highest any more, Wanda. Why not?' Wanda was experiencing the same optical illusion, and she could no more explain it than Liliane. 'It was extraordinary and deeply impressive – as though we had become the innermost centre of the Universe. It must have been wonderful to share a moment like that with a partner. I felt a little envious and rather sad.'

Wanda had not brought her heavy cine camera to the summit, but Maurice was carrying a little compact camera, and they took a lot of pictures. Soon the wind and the cold – it must have been -30°C to -40°C – became intolerable, and they began their descent, meeting two Basques from the Italian expedition on their way up to the summit. Wanda was first back to their 8300-metres bivouac, and decided to shelter from the wind for a brief rest. 'It was so bitterly cold outside. Just a few minutes' respite, I thought, and then I'll be ready to go on.'

Maurice was next, and as soon as he reached the tent he said, 'We'll stop here for the night.' Wanda agreed immediately, though she was well aware how dangerous it would be to spend a second night in the Death Zone, and realized that they were only postponing the dreaded descent. Descents were usually Wanda's strength but as she sat in the tent her thoughts were on the many outstanding climbers whose exhaustion on the way down from successful summit

climbs had led them into careless errors and to their deaths. 'Maurice was right. We were all very tired, and we needed some reserves of energy for those tricky stretches at the "Bottleneck".' Wanda was forgetting, however, that at such altitudes there can be no recovery. The human body can only deteriorate.

'We made a big mistake. When you climb without oxygen, success depends on your speed and how long you spend in the Death Zone. It was a terrible night. With no sleeping bags we sat miserably uncomfortable, shaking with cold and racked with anxiety. Sleep was impossible. In my physical and mental distress my intolerance of Michel and of his body touching mine became unbearable. And of course all these feelings were heightened by the altitude. I thought I might escape my pain and shorten the night by taking sleeping tablets, and took all of two-and-a-half Mogadon – with dreadful consequences. I felt sick and unpleasantly sleepy, but couldn't sleep. My limbs felt distant and leaden while my mind stayed all too active.'

Michel crawled out of the tent at first light. 'I'll go ahead and brew some tea', he said as he left. It was a formula that Wanda hated: the pretence of helpfulness, when all he

The snow shoulder above 8000 metres is so expansive that accurate orientation becomes impossible in bad weather.

Wanda after her successful ascent

wanted was to get away from a dangerous place as quickly as possible. Wanda, Liliane and Maurice struck the tent, so as to leave the mountain as they had found it. Wanda was still feeling quite dizzy from her sleeping tablets, but she set off next. She felt that Maurice and Liliane had enough problems looking after themselves and would not want to be in any way inhibited by her presence.

Michel was already too far below for contact, feeling his way down the ice traverse. Wanda realized that she could not depend on him for help but would have to rely on her own resources for the whole frightening descent.

'You can't afford the slightest slip at extreme altitude because there's no possibility of rescue. There's no way any partner could help you at 8000 metres, where minimal progress is all anyone can manage. All you can do is take great care and minimize your risks. This is when you have to admit that the extremes of mountaineering are no kindergarten but sport at its most dangerous.'

Suddenly Wanda heard a cry. Michel had fallen, was tumbling head over heels, faster and faster, down the 'Bottleneck', to land on a snow drift in front of the Basques' tents. To her astonishment, he stood up and trudged on down the mountain as though nothing had occurred. How many lives has a human?

Wanda inched her way safely down the ice terrace. At the 'Bottleneck' she found the descent easier than the way up since she could look down and be sure of her route. The following shoulder with its snow field also proved easier than she had feared, but at that point the weather suddenly turned ugly. The shoulder is a huge area of undifferentiated snow, totally featureless in bad visibility, and it was now almost impossible to find the way between the two crevasses to the snow bridge across the bergschrund. 'It was a miracle that I found it at all. I was conscious of how near I stood to death and yet, paradoxically, I didn't feel afraid. Instead of fear, I felt a marvellous, dream-like sense of inner

freedom. I was in a deluded state of euphoria produced by the sleeping pills I had taken; but another part of me was still properly aware of being on a dangerous descent in abominable weather, alone, unroped, exhausted and at the very limit of my resources. My sense of invulnerability was a danger, but it was also allowing me to function without physical inhibition and preserving me from panic. It saved my life by letting me climb to the utmost of my skills and permitting my luck to hold.'

Just before dropping down onto the steep rock face and the fixed ropes, Wanda looked up to see Maurice and Liliane in process of climbing through the 'Bottleneck', which meant that they should soon be on the shoulder below. Reassured, Wanda trudged on down to the great ice pinnacle where she had left her tent. She had still not properly recovered her sense of balance, even though she had taken a stimulant to counter the effects of the sleeping pills. As a result she felt simultaneously tense and sleepy, and so detached that the Basques overtook her without her even noticing. She reached her tent at 7700m about an hour after Michel, and the two sat waiting for Maurice and Liliane in their separate tents. Snow began to fall but still there was no sign of the Barrards.

Wanda wondered whether the sudden collapse of the weather had made them decide to bivouac on the snow shoulder. However, another night without sleeping bags would be a terrible ordeal, and Michel and Wanda were now becoming seriously alarmed. Michel made an attempt to walk towards them, but even the slightest ascent was now beyond his physical powers and visibility in the fog was down to less then five metres. Three Italians appeared and asked after Maurice and Liliane. Their response to Wanda's and Michel's tale was, 'We'll go up.' But Michel dissuaded them: 'There's no point. Visibility is zero.'

By next day it was clear that something had gone wrong. Wanda and Michel, now down to their last gas cartridge, could not go on waiting together. One of them would have to descend, and it was Wanda who decided to make the move. 'I asked myself whether there was any serious point in waiting any longer. It was mortally dangerous to stay on at that altitude. And I couldn't imagine coping with a serious crisis with Michel. When you're partnering an old and intimate friend you discover hidden reserves of energy, so that your performance can be out of all proportion to your limited strength. But the opposite is likely to be true if you're uncomfortable with your partner.'

The Italians decided to resume their descent and Wanda followed them, after picking up her ice-axe, which was helping to anchor her tent. She decided to leave the tent for the benefit of later expeditions. She struggled through the knee-deep snow, trying always to keep the Italians in sight in the thick mist since the snow in the wind was covering their tracks almost immediately. As she was negotiating an awkward little traverse, she suddenly saw her tent flying at her in the gale. Having torn itself from its site, it now narrowly avoided dragging Wanda to her death. She tried to secure enough footing to pull the poles out of the fabric, but had to give up and let the tent go on its way.

The Italians, seeing Wanda wrestling with her tent, assumed that she was setting up camp. They therefore continued their descent without, as they thought, needing to wait for her. Meanwhile she had lost her gloves while trying to deal with her tent and although she had second pair in reserve, they were very thin and offered little protection for her hands. Soon she heard voices, and the two ghostly figures who emerged out of the whiteness turned out to be the two Basques whom she had earlier encountered near the summit. The three Italians had long since disappeared from sight. At that moment she was delighted to come upon two ski poles stuck in the snow, thinking 'The Italians must have seen that I was finding the going hard and left them for me.' Almost desperate with cold and fatigue and at great risk of being ripped off the mountain by the storm, she made her way down the not-too-reliable old fixed ropes. Not until she had found her store tent in the new snow at the foot of the Black Pyramid did she feel safe. She sat down to wait for Michel, but with a new anxiety. She had realized, too late, that the two ski poles, so far from being intended for her, had actually been set to mark the entrance to the route down the face of the Black Pyramid. Their absence could spell death for Michel.

'How could I have been so irresponsible? It will be my fault if Michel doesn't make it. I hope to God nothing happens to him.'

Down at base camp a fearsome, dull, ominous, continuous roaring drove everyone there out of their tents. Although they could see nothing through the snow and fog, they knew it was the sound of gigantic, destructive avalanches hurling themselves down on to their glacier. Though they knew that the site of their camp was safe, the sheer thunderous volume of sound and the sensation of the first blast of the storm across the ice was enough to etch terror into their faces. The tents were billowing in the shock waves of the avalanches. Moments of absolute stillness alternated with yet louder thunders. Somewhere beyond the eerie white wall of fog, Nature had become a cacophony of rushing waterfalls and collapsing masses, as though the earth might be splitting apart. And indeed the whole glacier valley was flooding and its ice pinnacles crashing down as though they had never been.

The single thought in every mind was of their friends on the mountain. Radio messages were drowned by the noise of the winds and often all contact was lost. The storm was still raging the next day when a sort of walking icicle staggered into the camp, in the shape of Renato Casarotto. He had been forced to shelter for several days at 8000 metres on the 'Magic Line', and his superhuman exertions had terribly marked his features. He was followed into base camp a few hours later by the three Italians. As soon as Renato heard from them that the Barrards had vanished, he assembled an international rescue team in the hope, at least, of bringing down Wanda and Michel.

Gigantic avalanches hurling themselves down on to the glacier

Wanda found it too painful even to contemplate that the Barrards might be dead. She waited another day in her store tent, and another night, and then another day and night, still hoping against hope. In her loneliness she finally began to fear that she might be the group's only survivor – a crushing thought – and she realized that she could not survive much longer in the thin high air. She must lose no more time, but get back to base camp as soon as possible. She pulled some socks over her hands in place of the thin gloves, which had been Liliane's, and which she left in the store tent, still hoping that the others might yet be following. So she began to climb down, back to the land of the living, quickly and with no more stops, fearful of prolonging the destructive effects of altitude.

'Certain kinds of event only get to me much later, and I suppose this protects me from panic and probably saved my life. My reaction to aggression, disaster or tragedy is delayed. There are events that I have lived but still can't fully accept.'

Late that evening Wanda reached advanced base camp, which she found occupied by a group of Korean climbers and the rescue party, who had more or less given up hope of seeing her alive again, given the relentless

raging of the storm. Her joy at sipping mandarin juice in the company of the living doubled when she heard that Michel was still alive. He had waited and waited for his friends where Wanda had left him, but finally he too had decided he must opt for descent. He had reached 7200m and was at that very moment being directed by radio to the entrance into the Black Pyramid. Fortunately a French member of the Italian expedition could remember every detail of that section, and he gave Michel such clear directions that he was soon safely on the fixed ropes and into unambiguous terrain.

The last descending lap over the glacier found Wanda in real distress. One knee was very painful and her finger-tips were frostbitten. 'I'm not walking very convincingly, am I? I don't look much like a climber.' Her Polish friends offered to carry her rucksack, but her pride would not allow her to accept. 'No fear! I've been to the top of K2 and back. No one's carrying my rucksack but me!' Obstinately she trudged painfully on.

Base camp at last, and soon the American doctor was treating her frostbite and Willi Bauer was inspecting her knee. She was a pitiful sight, with pieces of skin hanging from her face and further, though less serious, frost-bite disfiguring her nose.

All hope had gone that Liliane and Maurice might be still alive. 'They had always kept quite close behind us and they'd had no

Wanda back at base camp with Austrian climber Sigi Wasserbauer

problems. They must have fallen, but it must all have happened so quickly that they didn't even have time to shout. And we just hadn't the strength to climb and try to find them.' Wanda and Michel were besieged by questioners, but were not talking to one another. 'He was too much of a "starlet", and he got on my nerves, always wanting to shine and be the centre of attention. But there's no question that he's an outstanding climber, and I've always been really sorry that I took those ski poles.'

Renato Casarotto was back on the mountain, inching his way up the 'Magic Line', supported at base camp by his wife Goretta and his friend Dr Arturio. Meanwhile Jerzy Kukuczka and Tadeusz Peotrowski were putting up high-altitude camps and store tents on the south face and were making good progress up the severe Sichel couloir route.

The other Polish expedition attempting the 'Magic Line' route also included three women – Krystyna Palmowska, Anna Czerwinska and Dobroslawa Miodowicz-Wolf. 'All three of them had been on K2 with me last time, and I was proud to see how independent they were now. They helped to build the high camps up this very difficult route, dragging incredible loads up the sheer ice and rock face like ants, working tirelessly to reach the summit of their dreams.'

Dobroslawa was everyone's darling at base camp, and in fact this was when she first got her nickname 'Mrówka' (ant). She had already decided that, should she fail on the 'Magic Line', she would risk a second, illegal, attempt by the Abruzzi Ridge.

Thus there were now three groups of Polish climbers on K2 – in three expeditions and on three different routes.

The next drama began with Kurt Diemberger sprinting across the glacier to the Casarottos' tent. 'Get on the radio fast, Goretta. I've been watching Renato speeding down from 8400m to keep ahead of the bad weather. He was down on to the bottom glacier, then he disappeared and hasn't re-appeared. He must have fallen into a crevasse.'

Renato had walked that same track across the glacier literally countless times, safely skirting this area of crevasse every single time. What had possessed him today to cut straight across? Goretta did her best to keep the panic out of her voice. 'We're coming. Kurt saw you disappear. For God's sake, hold on!' Waiting by the radio while rescuers set out was torture. It took them an hour to find the crevasse and lower a rope.

Although Renato had fallen all of forty metres, he managed to clip himself on and chimney upwards against the ice walls as he was being hoisted. It was a long business hauling him to the surface, and when he emerged his face was almost dead white and badly abraded. The rescuers laid him on a foam mat for the doctor to examine and gave him warm tea to drink, preparatory to carrying him carefully to base camp, but he died before they could move him.

A few days later Liliane Barrard's body was found, also on the lower glacier and presumably dragged off the mountain by an avalanche. Some of her fellow-climbers helped Wanda to bury Liliane by the Gilkey rock. 'I think Maurice and Liliane must have lost the route in the bad visibility and either fallen or been taken by surprise by an avalanche. I don't believe that they died of

Relieving the pain of frost-bite with a foot-bath

The Austrian climbers carrying Liliane Barrard's body down from the mountain.

exhaustion even though we were all feeling the effects of the altitude.'

As so often before and after, Wanda's doubts about allowing climbing to monopolize the centre of her life tormented her. 'Maybe no one should ever think of climbing as the be-all and end-all of life, but just as a recreation. It's as well that there aren't many people like me. Luckily there's still some order and normality out in the real world, whereas what I do is no use to anyone.'

The Austrians fixed ropes across the ice traverse, to protect the descent from the summit, ...

In August 1986 seven mountaineers, all climbing without oxygen, coincided at 8300m just below the summit of K2. Willi Bauer and Alfred Imitzer went to the summit. Hannes Wieser had had to turn round, and was waiting in the top camp for his friends' return. Alan Rouse also reached the summit that day; Dobroslawa Miodowicz-Wolf had to retreat just short of the summit. All five

were resting in the top camp. Kurt Diemberger and Julie Tullis, who reached the summit just before sunset, fell on their way down. Although they suffered no manifest injuries, they were forced to spend the night at 8500m in the open, dragging themselves back next day to the top camp, to join the others waiting for the snowstorms to end. It should have been their absolute priority to leave this extreme altitude, but they had not marked the route over the easier but deceptive terrain immediately below, even though all seven were aware of the altitude risk. Perhaps they felt there was safety in numbers, or perhaps they were already in the grip of altitude sickness. Either way, they stayed too long in the Death Zone.

Julie Tullis was the first to die – from the effects of her earlier fall. Hannes Wieser, Alfred Imitzer and Alan Rouse were already in the irrevocable throes of death and the

other three had no choice but to abandon them. They agreed that Willi Bauer was the quickest among them and that he should descend for help, digging out the fixed ropes as he went. 'Mrówka' was next but, lacking the right equipment, she was moving more slowly and Kurt overtook her. She died hanging from a fixed rope. She might perhaps have made it to safety had she not been alone, and Wanda was later bitterly to accuse Kurt of not giving her that chance. But nothing that Kurt Diemberger could have done, at the very limits of his own strength, could have saved her.

'All the climbers who were lost on K2 that year died because they stayed too long in the Death Zone, in spite of what, as top mountaineers, they all knew.' The symptoms of altitude sickness can take many forms. Climbers may overestimate their own abilities or resources. Altitude exhausts the body, inducing lethargy and death by inaction, hence the term 'Death Zone'. Oxygen deficiency destroys the human organism, causing weight loss and wasting of the muscles. The effects, taken together, are comparable to an accelerated rate of ageing.

The tragedies on K2 started a vigorous debate about the ethics of extreme mountaineering, particularly because the two Austrians Hannes Wieser and Alfred Imitzer had been still alive when they were abandoned on the mountain. But the facts were clear. They could not have been saved, and whoever might have stayed by their side would have died with them. 'These are dreadful decisions, and I wouldn't wish that situation on anyone.'

The media fastened on the tragedies, but said little about the achievements at the limits of mountaineering. The amazing 'Magic Line' route had been established. Wanda had been the first woman and the first Pole to the summit of K2, to be followed by two more women, both of whom died tragically in descent. Five climbers had reached the summit by difficult new routes, and no fewer than twenty-two by the Abruzzi Ridge. Eleven of these were members of expeditions climbing illegally, since the only Pakistani permits for the Abruzzi Ridge had gone to the Koreans, the Austrians and Wanda's expedition. In all, five Balti porters and twelve expedition

Wanda's solo attempt on Broad Peak helped her to come to terms with the tragedies of the K2 expedition

into a crevasse. Julie Tullis from Britain died of altitude sickness following a fall and a night in the open. Alan Rouse and the two Austrians Hannes Wieser and Alfred Imitzer died of exhaustion and altitude sickness. Five Balti porters were killed in crevasses, by rock-falls or from exposure. Only a few of those who died in 1986 have ever been found.

There was to be a comparable set of tragedies on the Abruzzi Ridge in 1995, when a group of seven were killed by an avalanche and two British climbers fell to their deaths. One of them – Alison Hargreaves – had been the first woman to climb Everest solo and without oxygen.

Within the parameters of her sport the conquest of K2 was perhaps Wanda's greatest achievement. 'But sorrow at the death of so many friends far outweighed any triumph I might have felt.' Three of Poland's top climbers were dead: Tadeusz Peotrowski, Wojciech Wroz and Dobroslawa Miodowicz-Wolf. 'I really liked them all, but "Mrówka" holds a special place in my memories and affections because we were such close friends at home as well as on the mountain.'

Another effect of the tragedies was to raise some questions about Wanda's climbing monomania. 'I needed to unwind the ferocity of my motivation, so I decided to go straight on to Broad Peak and attempt a solo alpine-style ascent, in spite of my frost-bitten fingers and the pain in my toes. The physical activity helped me come to terms with the deaths of my friends, but my body was still too weak. I was moving so slowly that I never even got as far as the first high camp.'

There remained the unfinished business of making a better grave for Barbara Kozlowska who had died on Broad Peak in 1985. Wanda had been given some money for this purpose by Barbara's family, and she tried to organize a local team to help her, but found that this was virtually impossible in a Muslim country where all infidel are perceived as unclean. As for the climbers at base camp,

members suffered fatal accidents. Twenty-seven summit conquests had cost seventeen lives.

Two Americans, John Smolich and Alan Pennington had perished in an avalanche. Maurice and Liliane Barrard were assumed to have fallen. Two Poles, Tadeusz Peotrowski and Wojciech Wroz, are thought to have been so exhausted after reaching the summit that they lost their crampons and fell. Dobroslawa Miodowicz-Wolf ('Mrówka') died of exhaustion. Renato Casarotto died from the injuries he sustained when he fell they were still in shock after the dreadful toll of misfortune. Enough was enough, and they wanted no more dangers.

Wanda's film footage had gone to ÖRF and they were the first TV network to broadcast reports of the dramatic and shocking events on K2. Wanda's material contained the last images of those who had not returned from K2 and the world's last sight of them, still talking happily. 'That's how we'll all remember them.' The footage was edited into two films about the expedition, of which one won first prize at the Graz Mountain Film Festival.

It was shortly after her success on K2 that I first met Wanda. I was working with Willi Bauer on his book *Light and Shade on K2* and I needed Wanda's view of what had happened. When we met in Munich she gave me a gripping account of her K2 expedition, to which my first reaction was astonishment that she could have achieved all this on her own, with no manager, no commercial sponsorship and no support of any kind beyond what she had been able to raise by her own efforts. Now Dr Marion Feik in Vienna had offered to become her agent and manager, and I strongly advised Wanda to accept. After some argument Wanda agreed – and Marion quickly became a central figure in Wanda's life.

K2 and Broad Peak from Concordia

Makalu
A losing race to the summit

Wanda's only true homes were base camps.

Wanda was back in the Himalayas at the beginning of September 1986, and in top form. Of the fourteen 8000-metre peaks she had as yet only scaled three, and her next challenge was to be Makalu in East Nepal, in what is still one of the most untamed regions in the world. Only the lowest levels of the valleys are inhabited, so the very long march to the mountain is the first of the many difficulties facing climbers. Wanda, whose previous experience had been mostly in the arid landscapes of Pakistan, was enchanted by the lush vegetation of East Nepal. She later declared that the dense rain-forest round the base of Makalu's ice-bound slopes were her favourite Himalayan landscape.

Dear Marion   6 September 1986
Your help in organizing this expedition was invaluable. I'm taking your perfume up to base camp, but I'll eat the ham on the approach march. I've left European civilization far behind and I'm enchanted by the landscape below Makalu. You really must come here one day – that is, if you're not scared of creatures that feed only on blood. (I don't know what they're called in German.) They're everywhere – in the grass, on the track, in the trees and bushes – on the alert for any animal or a human prey. We're plagued with rain and damp, as one always is on an expedition after the monsoon. We'll soon be getting into Sherpa territory, where the culture is Tibetan …

They marched in tropical heat and humidity and were plagued by the leeches which Wanda was unable to name in German. These unpleasant companions can squeeze through the eyelets of a boot or drop from a tree to suck themselves firmly into position somewhere on their victim.

At around 3000 metres civilization gives way to the solitude of the mountains. The track climbs steeply to the pass of Shipton La at 4200m and then leads over dangerous moraine screes. Wanda was climbing with an expedition led by Krzisztof Pankiewicz. He set up their base camp at around 5300m next to a group led by Reinhold Messner, who had set himself the aim of climbing all fourteen 8000-metre peaks and had already achieved twelve, leaving only Makalu and Lhotse.

Since Messner's decision two more climbers, Jerzy Kukuczka from Poland and Marcel Rüedi from Switzerland, had stated they also intended to climb the fourteen-peak set. 'We Poles seem to be particularly good at small alpine-style expeditions, new extreme routes and winter climbs', Kukuczka wrote to justify his ambition. The three men never implied any competition among themselves but the media, of course, had soon talked up a rivalry.

Dear Marion   14 September 1986
It's taken us until today to get up to base camp at 5300m. Our neighbours are

Reinhold Messner and his expedition. There's a very nice atmosphere. Marcel Rüedi and Professor Oswald Oelz are particularly positive and amusing. I've been ill with a throat and chest infection, but I've cured myself with antibiotics ...

Dear Marion   30 September 1986
The normal route up Makalu is not particularly difficult, but it is savagely strenuous. The high camps are a long way apart, which makes the ascent to the summit seem endless. One of the worst trials is having to keep retreading the track in deep snow, often up to your waist and burrowing like a mole. It's utterly exhausting work. I made it to about 8000 metres but by then I simply hadn't the strength to get any higher this time round. I think about you often, and I'm looking forward to your warm welcome in Vienna.

Reinhold Messner was impressed and delighted by Wanda's achievements, even though she had failed to reach the summit.

'Wanda is the living proof that women can put up performances at high altitude that most men can only dream of. I'm certain that a woman will have conquered the magic fourteen 8000-metre peaks within the next ten years.'

When Marcel Rüedi and Krzysztof Wielicki reached the final summit section Wielicki took a direct line to the summit and was soon back in the shelter of his tent at 7700m. But Marcel Rüedi was much slower to the summit and was forced to bivouac at 8200m with no tent or sleeping bag. Wielicki was very relieved, next morning, to see a dot moving down the mountain below the summit.

Reinhold Messner, Hans Kammerlander and Friedl Mutschlechner were also on their way to the summit that morning, and were keeping an eye open for Marcel Rüedi. Friedl Mutschlechner later described what happened. 'We should have met him coming down, but we didn't see him until we were a few hundred metres below the Poles' Camp III. He was sitting in the snow, leaning with his hands on his ski poles as though he were taking a little rest. But he was dead. His iron will was a by-word, and he'd conquered eleven 8000-metre peaks. We simply could not understand it.'

Ewa Pankiewicz, who became Wanda's favourite climbing partner

Priceless advantages accrue when different expeditions can co-operate.

*Base camp, against
the back-drop of
Makalu*

The three climbers from the Italian Tirol reached the summit – Reinhold Messner's thirteenth 8000er – on 26 September 1986. Back at base camp, Messner and Hans Kammerlander decided that they could capitalize on their high degree of altitude acclimatization by heading straight for Lhotse.

Meanwhile Kukuczka had organized an international two-peak expedition which he hoped might keep him in the race to achieve the set of 8000-metre hills. Their aim was to climb Manaslu (8163m) – to add it to his score but also as acclimatization for an immediate assault on the extreme south face of Annapurna.

'A terrible hurricane held us prisoner in the snow, with the wind and the extreme cold almost driving us mad. What we had intended as a quick dash to the summit turned into endless days of purgatory,' was Kukuczka's later description.

All the while Reinhold Messner was edging steadily towards the fulfilment of his dream. Lhotse was to be his fourteenth and Kammerlander's seventh 8000-metre peak. In Messner's account, 'The weather was terrible, but Hans just climbed and climbed. If he'd even so much as hesitated, I'd have turned straight round and headed down with him. We never even stopped when we got to the point on the summit. We were much too frightened of being swept down by the wind to want to stop and savour our triumph. Anyway, no ascent is a success until after the descent is safely done.'

Thus on 16 October 1986 Reinhold Messner became the first man to have stood on every mountain over 8000 metres – on all the fourteen highest points on our earth. Messner afterwards always maintained that his most remarkable achievement was not to have climbed the peaks but to have returned safe to base camp each time. Kukuczka had lost the race: 'Of course I was a bit sad, but it was a great relief to be free to take my own time, now that the public pressure was off me.'

Annapurna in winter

'Climbing had become as basic to my life as sleeping and eating. However well I might feed my appetite, I was soon hungry again. I'd developed a real addiction …' Following the failed attempt on Makalu in the winter of 1986/7, Wanda wanted to link up with Jerzy Kukuczka to attempt Annapurna, but there was a snag. The expedition had been mysteriously struck off the record in Kathmandu, but the Poles were undaunted. While Wanda and Jerzy pushed baksheesh round the necessary offices, the other expedition members marched as quickly as they were able to establish a base camp.

Dear Marion   11 January 1987
We're waiting to fly from Pokhara to Jomoson, but the little local planes can't take off in bad weather. We're sure to be on our way to Annapurna in the next few days, even if we don't yet know just when. I was busy in Kathmandu working the system to get more permits for the future. I just can't slow down, even in Nepal. I've had a better idea for the Kukuczka film. I'm going to make the analogy between the race for the fourteen peaks and the race for the North Pole, even though this mountain race is a pure media invention.

Base camp was ready on 20 January but their winter permit was only valid until 15 February. A solid wall of ice at the base of the north face seemed to present an insuperable obstacle but they found a possible, moderately secure route between rock walls on the left of the face.

Kukuczka has given us his account: 'When we needed to rope up, it happened that Wanda and I were partnered. Now Wanda is an exceptional woman, totally fit. But I still have to confess that I hate climbing with women and if I can avoid collaborating on the mountain with a woman, I do.'

Four climbers began this fiercely difficult ascent – Wanda and Jerzy in one team, Krzysztof Wielicki and Artur Hajzer in the other. They first had to climb a steep, avalanche-prone couloir, then continue upwards on ice so hard that their crampons would not bite. The cold was terrible and they were climbing under an almost continuous hail of ice slivers and rock splinters, which even drilled holes through their tents. After two dreadful nights Wanda and Krzysztof knew that they had not sufficiently acclimatized and perforce gave up, leaving Kukuczka and Hajzer to carry on to spend the next night at 7700m. The following morning

Jerzy Kukuczka at base camp

the weather was even worse. The only way they could make progress was by following radio instructions from their friends at base camp – who were guiding them from photographs. Miraculously and notwithstanding all these difficulties, they not only made it to the summit but returned safe and sound to base camp.

Thus Jerzy Kukuczka's expedition ended in success after sixteen days. Wanda and Krzysztof made one more summit attempt, but had to give up when Wanda contracted a nasty bronchitis – as do so many Himalayan mountaineers: the air at high altitude is extremely dry, making the respiratory passages vulnerable to infection.

'Expeditions are hard work. To experience the beauty of these mountains you have to learn to perform beyond the apparent limits of your own body. My senses are at their most alert to the vivid impressions when I am physically and mentally drained. I often contract throat infections, but I don't talk about them. I believe in drugs, so I simply medicate myself. The clean air of the mountains soon restores your body. That's why I believe it's best to move on from one mountain to the next as quickly as possible, rather than return home between climbs to the unhealthy city air.'

Dear Marion   18 February 1987
The events of the last three weeks seem quite straightforward when I sit and write them down, but in fact I have survived some of the worst perils of my life. The route on Annapurna was a very dangerous one. Jerzy Kukuczka and Artur Hajzer made it to the summit on 3 February. I felt I hadn't had time to acclimatize and decided to wait for a few more

Wanda's attempt was foiled by snow-storms.

95

days – and paid the price. I never got to the summit, although I got to Camp II on 6 February, Camp III at 6150m on 7 February and Camp IV at 6800m on 8 February. But I was in poor condition, with a bad cough. I did shoot a lot of film, and if it's good material I shall be satisfied …

Thank you for remembering my birthday. We left base camp on 12 February and got to Kathmandu yesterday. I have to be in Warsaw on 20 February and go straight on to do some filming in Zakopane. Then, on 1 March I have to go to Milan with Kukuczka and Wielicki to do a TV programme. The 'Gazetta dello Sport' have organized a discussion with Messner. After that I'll be working on films back in Poland with ÖRF.

Returning home is not the end of an expedition. Much work remains to be done: lectures to be given, reports to write, accounts to close off, film and photographs to be catalogued and marketed. 'My photos are a prime source of income, worth many times their weight in gold, but even that is revenue which comes at the cost of the duplicate transparency – so much more expensive in Poland than in the West – that I have to send out before I can claim my reproduction fee.'

Wanda's home was a tenth-floor flat in a building on Sobieskego Street in Warsaw with a choice view over smoking factory chimneys. The hall was stacked with rucksacks, ropes and karabiners, the walls hung with photos and paintings of Himalayan mountains and expeditions. Every room harboured yet more climbing equipment, every bookshelf was crammed with climbing guides for every corner of the globe, every horizontal surface was buried under maps and pictures. The mountains were ubiquitous.

'When I'm at home I appreciate all the normal comforts which I have to do without on expeditions, but ordinary people take for granted. I'm by no means a nature freak, but a city person at heart. That's one of the contradictory things about me. I couldn't live on a desert island because I'm far from modest in my tastes. I love stylish clothes, elegant furnishings, quality cars and the like.'

Wanda began to organize her flat as a

working office. The Polish telephone system had always been a problem – even domestic calls were unreliable, never mind international communications. Finally things improved and she acquired a reliable line. 'Nowadays I can organize an expedition just by exchanging a few faxes. Until recently conditions here made it all so difficult: not only raising money, but even fixing dates and rendezvous. It only takes a tiny ambiguity to make big problems later when the expedition is under way. I've had some very bad experiences of that kind.'

Wanda's periods at home were always too short. She always took on too much, and the planning of her schedules always ended in chaos and stress, even after Marion had begun to help with preparations. The biggest problem was the hunt for sponsors. 'I struggle with that because I'm basically shy. Getting the money together for an expedition is much harder than battling to the summit. I'm so busy with administration that I hardly have time to get into the mountains and often end by running or doing strength training in the

gym at the Polish Climbers' Club.'

When Marion first met her, Wanda was managing to live on $1000 a month, which included a lot of expenses which, though essential, were enormous by Polish standards. Saving for the future was out of the question. 'Of course lots of people thought that climbing Everest had made me into a millionairess.'

Her life was becoming more and more pressurized, with virtually no leisure and sometimes too little time even for sleep. 'Maybe I'll go back to my profession one day. I feel quite nostalgic about it sometimes. I haven't worked at the Institute in Warsaw since 1982, but I've never broken my connection and I still feel a link to it.' But these were mere dreams. Wanda knew how much the world of computer science had changed and that there was no going back.

'I live for the mountains, but I don't live only by the mountains. I'm not just a climber, and I don't ever want to be just a climber. I've devoted a lot of the last few years to mountaineering, but I'd like to be more than just a good climber. My one guiding principle for both the mountains and the other parts of my life is to be good enough to do my own achieving.'

A 'city person at heart'? Wanda on the mountain, and at work in Warsaw

Shisha Pangma

Throne of the Gods

Wanda went to Shisha Pangma in summer 1987 with Jerzy Kukuczka. Theirs was the first Polish expedition to brave the lengthy negotiations with the Chinese for a permit, and it included Elsa Avila and Carlos Carsolio from Mexico, Christine de Colombel and Malgorzata Bilczewska-Fromenty from France, Alan Hinkes from Britain, Steve Untch from the USA, Ramiro Navarette from Ecuador, and the Poles Artur Hajzer, Dr Lech Koriszewski, Janusz Majer and Riszard Warecki.

Dear Marion   12 August 1987
You know why I owe you this 'thank you'. The gas arrived just two hours before I had to leave. I'd begun to think there'd be only cold drinks on this expedition. The ham is delicious ... Shisha Pangma is right on the border with Nepal, so we had thought the quickest way would be by bus and truck to the fron-tier post at Kodari. But the road had been damaged by landslides so the trip took two days instead of eight hours, and we all had to walk, with the porters carrying our equip-ment. From the border, the Chinese provided transport to base camp. Everything about this expedition is very different from climbing through Pakistan and Nepal. The hotel at the frontier was like a barracks, with rooms like prison cells. Next day we were driven straight up to 5000 metres, which made us all feel pretty awful. Then, to our surprise our accompanying officer suddenly ordered the trucks to stop and unload. You could just see the peaks in the distance, but the officer insisted that it would be dangerous to estab-lish our base camp any higher ...

Most base camps for 8000-metre ascents are pitched at about 5000 metres because this is a good altitude both for altitude acclimatization and for recuperation from the debilitating labour higher on the mountain. The Chinese

---

The icy mass of Shisha Pangma rises to 8046m out of a barren, ochre plateau. The Tibetan nomads call it 'The ridge over the high pastures'. The Sanskrit name is Gosainthan –'The throne of the gods'. It was the last 8000-metre summit to fall, lying so far north in the forbidden territory of Tibet.

In 1964 the Chinese built a track to the foot of the mountain at 5900 metres. A huge, 200-strong expedition led by Hsu Ching was transported to the head of this track on a fleet of jeeps and trucks. They spent several months in their base camp, which even had a cinema, and ten Chinese and Tibetan climbers finally reached the summit by way of the north-west face and the north ridge on 2 May.

Shisha Pangma was opened to foreigners in 1980, when a German and an Austrian expedition were successful.

In 1981 Junko Tabei, the first woman to climb Everest, leading a Japanese women's expedition, became the first woman to reach the summit. In the same year Reinhold Messner and Friedl Mutschlechner also managed a success-ful ascent in weather of extreme severity.

In 1982 a British expedition led by Doug Scott climbed the south face, which had been considered unclimbable, with neither fixed ropes nor high-altitude camps. In the autumn of that year all six members of a Japanese expedition led by Makoto Hara reached the summit by the Chinese route.

In 1989 Pavle Kozjek and Andrej Stremfelj put up a new extreme route on the south wall. In 1990 Wojtek Kurtyka, Erhard Loretan and Jean Troillet reached the Central Summit by a new route and in their special style – climbing by night with ultra-light packs and no tents.

Organized expeditions increasingly became the rule during the next few years. Shisha Pangma is regarded as the easiest of the 8000-metre peaks and as such is very popular. Many nationalities are represented among those who have reached the top, but not all those who have made the attempt have returned alive.

had followed this practice on Shisha Pangma, but here the foot of the mountain was at least 40km away and the original track was no longer viable. If the expedition was to have any chance of success, their base camp would have to set nearer to the action.

Over two days the expedition members dragged themselves to the base of the mountain, while their equipment made the trek on yaks. Finally base camp was established on a site close to the foot of the mountain that would avoid the need for long approach work, but at an altitude, 5900 metres, at which the human organism deteriorates for lack of oxygen.

Janusz Majer was the first to suffer; his speech became confused and his legs would no longer hold him up. 'We gave him oxygen and made a stretcher with skis to get him down as quickly as possible.' It was a laborious business, but Janusz's altitude sickness

only lasted a few days, and he was soon back at base camp.

On 30 August Kukuczka, Hajzer, Hinkes and Untch made a reconnaissance on skis to the summit of Jebokalgan-Ri, 7200m, next to Shisha Pangma. After this the whole team set about building their high-altitude camps, not without encountering some dangers, as when one group was nearly blown off the mountain by the pressure wave of an avalanche that passed over their heads.

A few days later the weather turned and continuous heavy snow forced the whole expedition to sit idle at base camp for ten days. They began to fear that their permitted time would run out before they could mount a summit ascent, but Kukuczka managed to negotiate five extra days with their Chinese officer – to 25 September.

'With 13 members, a mixture of men and women and six nationalities we had been

The Chinese camp at the road-head at 5000 metres is more than 40km from Shisha Pangma.

Wanda on the track to the 5900m base camp

prophesied a lot of problems, but they never materialized. There was no segregation of tasks by gender. And anyway I won't stand for anyone on any expedition assuming I'm going to do the cooking because I'm a woman.' But no one has any chance of getting near the kitchen when Jerzy Kukuczka is on a team. He never cooks at home, but loves to cook on expeditions.

On 16 September 1987 the weather improved and, as everyone was now well acclimatized, the whole team raced off. 'Some of them were in such a hurry that they forgot their sleeping bags', Kukuczka told me afterwards with a shake of his head. 'I heard over the radio that Wanda and the Mexicans were intending to skip the top camp to get to the summit first. Exceptionally for me, I pulled rank as leader and stopped them because of the extra risk involved. Meanwhile Artur and I left the normal route at 6800m to open a new one to the summit along the crest of the west ridge. We had no problems along the way, bivouacked for the second night at

7200m, after which the terrain got tougher and, recognizing that the final ridge to the summit is both very long and dotted with a lot of rock towers some of which have to be climbed, we bivouacked for a third night at 7900m.'

At about 3 p.m. on 19 September Carlos Carsolio was first to reach the summit, followed by several other Shisha Pangma firsts: Ramiro, first Ecuadorian; Elsa, youngest woman; and Wanda, first Pole, just as she had been on Everest and K2.

'It's only on the last metres of an ascent, that I start to enjoy the feeling that I'm going

The spectacular ice-fall at the foot of Shisha Pangma

Shisha Pangma's long summit ridge

to succeed. It's a wonderful moment, when I feel utterly exhausted and utterly happy at the same time. I'm delighted to have another damned peak over and done with, but that moment at the summit is also the end of something – the signal to turn about and begin to return to ordinary life. Whenever you achieve something, you're standing at the end of another road …'

Kukuczka, on his skis, was the last to the summit, and with it the fulfilment of his dream of the whole set of 8000-metre peaks. The next day he skied all the way back to base camp. When he got home a telegram was waiting for him, from Reinhold Messner, which read, 'You're not number two. You're magnificent.'

Wanda had filmed and photographed the whole expedition, including some remarkable shots of the 8000-metres-high summit ridge. 'Photography has become my second passion. It's so creative, like looking at the world through a magnifying glass. Maybe I'll

take it up professionally when I'm too old to climb.'

Wanda on the summit

Cerro Torre
A Patagonian
adventure

Patagonia – every climber's dream destination

The magnificent granite pinnacle of the Cerro Torre is crowned by a gigantic block of ice in the shape of a mushroom. Every few years it breaks off, only to form again. There is nothing like it on any other mountain in the world. Wanda was tempted to Patagonia and the Cerro Torre by photographs which showed that an attempt would be a welcome break from trudging through deep Himalayan snow. She set out in December 1988 to try her luck, with Ewa Szczesniak, Iwona Gronkiewicz-Marcisz, Monika Niedbalska and her friend Ewa Pankiewicz. 'Ewa had become my favourite climbing partner.' They had shared all sorts of climbing adventures and developed a satisfying compatibility.

The base camp for Cerro Torre stands in a little wood, a few hours walk from the foot of the rock. When they got there, the Polish women found themselves in the company of top climbers from all over the world, including Wolfgang Müller from Germany, Hans Kammerlander from the Italian Tirol, Carlos Buhler and Jim Bridwell from the USA and

It was in the Patagonian summer of 1957/8 that two rival Italian groups – one led by Bruno Detassis, the other by Walter Bonatti – made the first attempt on the Cerro Torre, known as 'the hardest mountain on earth'. A year later Cesare Maestri who had been a member of the Detassis team returned to the Cerro Torre with Toni Egger and they reached the summit by the north face. On the way down Toni Egger was swept away by a snow-and-ice avalanche and Maestri returned alone, to doubts whether he had indeed reached the top.

Maestri returned in 1970 to force the famous Maestri route over the east ridge, and fixed some protection on the final vertical granite slabs to the summit. 30 metres below the summit he fixed his compressor to a bolt, removed some parts to make it unusable and then broke off all the other bolts from there to the summit. All this in order to demonstrate that the final pitch was impossible without artificial aids. Moreover by pioneering a different route for his second attempt Maestri further deepened the mystery surrounding his earlier climb.

Jim Bridwell – a top American climber – was the next to the summit, but that was not until 1979. Bridwell fixed tiny aluminium clips – strong enough to serve as holds but not as protection in the event of a fall – and hammered wedges into tiny cracks. His hardware is still being used today.

In 1987 Rosanna Manfrini, climbing with her friend Maurizio Giordani, was the first woman to the summit.

In 1988 Wanda and her companions were the first women's rope to make the attempt.

Silvo Karo and Stianec Jegic from Yugoslavia. They were all waiting for climbable weather conditions; some of them had been waiting for weeks. It rained for days on end, snowed almost continuously and blew a storm most of the time, but it was never very cold. The Polish women celebrated a proper Polish Christmas with a traditional dinner and authentic Christmas cake.

Beside the foot of the Maestri route there is a snow cave where most climbers spend the night before their attempt in order to make an early start. The weather on the Cerro Torre is totally unpredictable and constantly changing. Apparent improvements are often only fleeting. It is a rare privilege to get even a glimpse of the mountain. The moment a rope decides to move up to the snow cave, all the other waiting climbers follow to be quite sure of not missing any possible chances.

'We decided to try our luck in spite of the poor weather and the wintry conditions on the great granite face, so off we went, saying that the weather was so bad, it could only improve.' A thin layer of snow covered the rock. It was not too difficult to fix protection on the lower pitches, but it became very difficult higher up where there were only a few old pitons on a Grade VI vertical wall with overhangs.

Patagonia did its best to live up to its reputation as the land of storms. The weather went from terrible to catastrophic, with drifting snow and fog making it impossible to see the route. When the rock had disappeared under deep new snow and their speed reduced almost to zero they had to admit defeat. Kammerlander and Müller made the summit, but none of the other groups on the mountain that year could follow them.

Christmas in the 'waiting room' at the foot of Cerro Torre

As the climbers gain height, the climbing becomes more difficult.

Yalung Kang First encounter with Kanchenjunga

Wanda mounted her first attempt on a Kanchenjunga peak – Yalung Kang (8505m) – in the winter of 1988/9, setting out with six men from Wroclaw, two academics from Göttingen in West Germany and Ewa Pankiewicz to put up a new route. 'If Ewa and I reach the summit, we'll be the first women ever to have climbed an 8000-metre peak in winter.'

Kanchenjunga stands at the easternmost tip of Nepal, right on the border with Sikkim. From the Nepalese capital Kathmandu to the nearest roadhead is a fourteen-hour bus ride, and from there the approach is on foot. Stores and equipment have to be carried by porters who can carry loads up to 80kg supported by a head-band across the forehead. Even young boys and girls offer to toil for six to ten hours a day as porters.

The track leads through terraced fields, over hill-top ridges, past waterfalls, through dramatic gorges, round dangerous landslides and over primitive bamboo bridges. Tiny dwellings perch high on the valley slopes likes eagles' nests. At 3410m, among dense rhododendrons and conifers hung with orchids and lianas, there is a pool called Torantan. Here the porters halt, to sleep in a cave beside the pool. The forest here is sacred; no beast may be slaughtered. A tiny Buddhist temple cut into the rock is dedicated to Devi Than, the goddess of the forest. In the faith of the inhabitants of the valley it is held that praying here once a year ensures the fulfilment of wishes and that the spirits of those who die here will for ever inhabit the mountains.

The houses in the last village look rather

The Kanchenjunga massif, with its numerous peaks, is sometimes known as 'The treasure-house of the snows'. The highest are: the main summit, which is also the third-highest in the world (8595m); middle summit (8482m); south summit (8476m); west summit, also known as Yalung Kang (8505m); and Jannu (7710m). The full name, being not the easiest to pronounce, is often abbreviated to 'Kanch'.

Douglas Freshfield achieved his legendary circuit of the base of Kanchenjunga as early as 1899.

In 1929 a German expedition led by Paul Bauer reached 7400 metres on the north-east spur. In 1930 an international expedition under the leadership of G.O. Dyhrenfurth failed at 6400 metres, at the cost of the life of one Sherpa, buried in an ice avalanche.

Paul Bauer led another German expedition in 1931 which reached 7700 metres, again on the north-east spur. One Sherpa and H. Schaller fell to their deaths, and another Sherpa died of illness.

The summit finally fell on 25 May 1955, to Joe Brown and George Band, two members of a British expedition led by Charles Evans, climbing the Yalung face from Nepal. They were followed next day by Tony Streather and Norman Hardie. All four men refrained from standing on the precise summit in deference to the religious beliefs of their hosts.

In 1977 an Indian expedition led by Colonel Narender Kumar reached the main summit by the north-east ridge.

Three British climbers – Doug Scott, Peter Boardman and Joe Tasker – made the third summit ascent in 1979, via the north col and without oxygen.

In 1980 a Japanese expedition opened another route to the summit up the north face.

In 1982 Reinhold Messner and Friedl Mutschlechner pioneered a route on the north flank.

In 1983 Joe Bachler from Austria soloed from the top camp to the summit by the south-west flank, and Pierre Beghin managed the same feat completely solo.

A Japanese expedition of 1984 made the traverse of the South, Central and Main Summits.

In 1991 Andrej Stremfelj and Marko Prezelj, with no advance reconnaissance, climbed the awesome south ridge.

Kanchenjunga was not climbed by a woman until May 1998, when Briton Ginette Harrison reached the top.

Kanchenjunga group from the approach march

like the shepherds' huts on the high summer meadows of the Alps, with wooden roof trusses built on to stone walls and covered with stone shingles. Prayer flags flutter in the wind in front of each house. Herds of cattle roam through the conifers and rhododendrons, the orchids and lichens all the way up to Lake Lapsang and the two stone huts on the meadow of Ramze at 4620m. In the village all the expedition equipment is loaded onto yaks for the next stage of the approach march, via Oktang to the Yalung glacier.

Wanda's team had been on the march for two weeks when they reached the site for their base camp, in an amphitheatre of glacier, rock and seracs.

Day after day Wanda and her partner fought their way up and down, through the deep snow and up the steep icy rocks, but the weather was so bad and the danger from avalanches so extreme that their best efforts could get them no higher than 7000 metres and they were forced to admit defeat.

'I take all my emotions to the mountains with me, so any fighting I do is with myself, not the mountain. Sport is a good way of externalizing your pent-up aggressions; you can direct your competitiveness at the tough business of survival. What you can't do is dominate the mountain. Mountains never forgive mistakes, which is why I keep up a dialogue with them. On Yalung Kang fear was

An isolated peasant house on the approach track

105

Yalung Kang from Oktang, above the Yalung glacier

our constant companion and our counsellor if we needed to assess our capacities. Fearlessness is a kind of deficiency. Whenever I couldn't see all my partners I felt an overwhelming loneliness. You don't have to be icy cool and fearless, but you do have to control your fears and get in direct contact with Nature or God's creation. When I'm up in that thin air, suffering at every step, I'm able to reach deep into my inner self and in those moments I have a certainty that someone is helping me. Perhaps it's just my mother praying for me at home, but it may truly be the presence of God.'

Wanda actively enjoyed extreme situations on the mountain. To set out on expedition meant a return to familiar routines, and some welcome leisure for inner contemplation. By contrast the rush and movement of her ground-level life often made her long for the quiet of her little tent. 'That's when I get the

chance to read and think. I lie there, relishing the Beethoven on my Walkman sounding over the noise of the storm outside.' Wanda always kept faith with her passion and her personal ambitions.

I next met Wanda soon after her return from Kanchenjunga. We had been climbing, and were lying in the sunshine making plans. Wanda was trying to persuade me to join an expedition to another of her 8000-metre peaks.

'Wanda,' I insisted, 'I'm quite content to do my gazing at 8000-metre peaks from below. I've cycled and trekked in India and Nepal, and sometimes even climbed onto summits – though not because I thought it was vital to do so – and I've sometimes done these things at altitudes above 6000 metres where I've felt almost eyeball-to-eyeball with some of the giants. I'm boundlessly curious and my curiosity often drives me out in search of new places and new people. Sometimes I find somewhere I particularly like and stay a while. I've learned how little I need to be content, even happy. The life of the people of the Himalaya has made them independent of all that is inessential, and I'm infinitely more fascinated by their faith and the mysteries of their culture than I am by climbing. I like the nomadic life. There's no room for illusions on the roof of the world. Even when you're only a tourist you begin to understand how hard it is to live in the lands of the Himalaya and survive. The land and its people have taught me to exist on less and cut down my baggage to the bare minimum. Nowadays the less I drag around and the less of any value I have to worry about at home, the freer I feel.'

Wanda was baffled by my arguments, and replied: 'You're forgetting that there's something quite exceptional about climbing an 8000-metre peak. It's an intense adventure even if you're familiar with the route. Your situation on the mountain changes from hour to hour; success is never sure, and usually depends on the weather and the avalanches. You're a good climber. You've planned and organized climbing tours and you've led some difficult routes. Why don't you want to come?' If she had only known how I had longed in the past to be invited on to an expedition, and never dared even to dream of climbing with the famous Wanda Rutkiewicz. But since then my dreams and ambitions had changed.

I could only answer, 'I climb for pleasure. Expeditions are serious enterprises, and very expensive. What am I supposed to do for money? I need to put in a lot of work just to keep myself, which doesn't leave much time for training. It would be such a much more expensive hobby than I could ever afford. I'd need sponsors, which would mean publicizing myself, and I hate public speaking and self-promotion. It makes me so nervous that I struggle to say my piece at all.'

'But the publicity wouldn't do you any harm in your professional journalism and authoring. I'll get the equipment together. The expedition is being organized for us by the Polish Academies' Mountaineering Association, so it won't cost us very much. It's not happening until the summer of 1990, so you've got lots of time. Meanwhile I'll be on Gasherbrum II in 1989 with a British women's expedition, and you could pay me a visit at base camp there.'

I was not much attracted by the idea of a trip into the Karakorum or of travel among the down-trodden women of Muslim Pakistan. However Marion, Wanda's friend and manager, would be going, and as she is not a climber I was concerned for her safety and welfare. I had come to admire Marion's capacity to deal calmly with situations and problems that would have driven others to despair, and I had grown very fond of her. And so, finally, I agreed to Wanda's proposition.

Ewa, partnering Wanda once again

Gasherbrum II

First British all-women expedition

In 1989 Wanda joined the British women's expedition to Gasherbrum II. A British TV programme had asked her to film for them, but their proposed contract was only for delivery of unedited material, whereas Wanda wanted to shape her own film. At the very last moment she was able to arrange an alternative deal on her own terms with RIAS–Berlin.

'This was to be one of my happiest expeditions.' The group included married women and mothers, in fact the British Mountaineering Club leader Brede Arkless had no fewer than eight children. She had had four with her husband, then separated and had four more with her present partner. She and the two men together had a business running climbing and mountain training courses. 'I admire the way that Brede has broken out of convention. She's managed to combine family, climbing and a good, if a little motherly, relationship with her two men.'

Women must be veiled except in their own homes.

Wanda's plan was to go on after the end of the expedition to the Broad Peak base camp, to give Barbara Kozlowska, who had died on the mountain in 1985, a proper burial at last. Marion Feik, a geologist friend Leonore Hoke and I had agreed to meet Wanda at the base camp to help her with the task.

Dear Marion   4 June 1989
I hope you're well and setting out soon for Pakistan. I'm already looking forward to seeing you, though it'll be a while yet. Hotels in Rawalpindi are cheap and interesting. We stayed at the Park Hotel in Murray Road, but you'd have no problem in finding somewhere even cheaper. I've had endless problems with the Ministry of Tourism, who seem to be able to turn anything into a crisis. It's hard work forcing your way through the endless bureaucracy. The English women have been at base camp since 30 May, but I'm hoping to get there only a week later, unless more problems develop here.

Get in touch with my friend Nazir Sabir in Islamabad. He was the second Pakistani with us on K2. He'll arrange everything and not charge you, but unfortunately he's difficult to get hold of. I've suggested Ali Chedar, from Satpara as your Sirdar. He's just about to accompany me to base camp, and he's reliable. He'll meet you at the K2 Hotel in Skardu where the manager is fully au fait. Rates have doubled since 1986. Porterage to base camp is now about $100 per porter, and you have to reckon 50 to 60 per cent more baggage than your own because the porters also have to carry the food you provide for them.

All my best wishes   Wanda

Pakistan comes at you like some huge firework display. There are plenty of oriental towns with bazaars, but the bazaars of Rawalpindi outstrip them all. The perfume of foods and spices pervades the hot streets. Fruit sellers wipe their wares in a constant battle against the dust that blows in every breeze. Towering stacks of metal vessels and ceramic pots seem to defy gravity. Craftsmen can just be made out, at work in little court-yards. Goldsmiths' ornaments shimmer in glass display cases and windows. Behind the crooked walls of the pale yellow and blue and pink houses dark-skinned, wild-eyed Afgh-ans are selling antique silver ornaments and Kalashnikovs. The streets outside are alive with seething humanity, rent by the cacopho-ny of cassette recorders, and watched over by Arabic inscriptions and the lapis-lazuli blue ceramics on the minaret of the mosque, where only men are permitted to pray. Fig-ures hurry along the streets in proud and fluid motion, their faces brown and framed with black beards and glistening hair, their bodies elegant in their flowing clothes. Pakistan is a land made for men.

Just a step from the mysteries of the bazaar lies the raucous, hectic bedlam of the main streets, a seething mass of honking, over-crowded buses, trucks and collective taxis, all decorated with bright paints, garish decals, mirror fragments, feathers and gleaming plaques of beaten metal. Heavy chains and bells clank from the undersides as they roar by. Every vehicle seems to have to prove its existence by the hand pressed permanently on the horn. The average driver's view of the road is limited to a single peep-hole through the flowers and the paper decorations that obscure most of the windscreen. Perhaps the only way to cope with the anarchy of the road is not to be able to see it.

Herds of sheep, goats and fat water buf-faloes trot along toward the river in an envi-able display of jay-walking through the cli-mactic hues and the slurried streets of the heaving city. They seem oblivious of every-thing and everybody around them. Even the packed buses and collective taxis, lumbering off on their often long and always overladen journeys with their human cargo hanging off them like grapes, can not disturb these beasts. Comment on all this to a local, and the reply, with a shrug, will be, 'Ah, yes! Rush hour in Pindi!'

Dear Marion   *21 June 1989*
The weather has been bad for the whole of the last two weeks, which is particularly annoying as the Swiss ahead of us had such good weather that they were up and down in ten days. Whereas we've not yet got any high-er than Camp I at 6000m. I'm a bit worried that you may not have received all my letters, so I'm having this one delivered to the Hotel Skardu by hand. In my last letter I set out the porters' stages for every day of the approach march. I hope you and Gertrude have arrived safely. I'm looking forward to seeing you.
  Kisses Wanda

The women did all they could to make life at base camp enjoyable through the long days of bad weather. The Pakistani officers accom-panying the various expeditions built a huge snow-woman with big breasts. 'We respond-ed with a gigantic snowman with every work-ing part shaped with loving care. I filmed the whole performance and we all had a good laugh. The Pakistanis were so shocked that

The expedition's guide, Ali Chedar

Marion on the rope bridge

The English climbers building their snow-man at base camp

they had to look away every time they walked past him. I've never had so much fun on an expedition.'

Wanda wanted her film to give a true picture of a women's expedition rather than some idealized drama played by immaculate, laughing heroines and stoical martyrs bowed down by the mighty winds. She shot sequences of the climbers washing their hair, repairing their make-up, joking, playing around, hanging their washing out in their snow hut, discussing plans, cooking and lying snug in their tents.

Other sequences showed a different side of the same women: in blizzards, dangling from fixed ropes over fearsome crevasses, treading tracks across ultra-steep slopes, struggling through horrid terrains under huge rucksacks, unrecognizable with their hair and goggles encrusted with ice. 'And of course I also took some of the shots you would expect: the glittering crests of the Karakorum, the riven glaciers, the sheer cliffs and the thread of our insignificant track in the immensity of the snow.'

Wanda's 'Snow-women' is the only film ever to have made something gripping out of the ordinary details of life on an expedition. It is not technically perfect – none of Wanda's films is that – but it is unique. No one before or since has so well caught the

contrast between these women's happy confidence at rest and the tensions and dramas they have to face on the mountain. But the film won no prizes. 'I think "Snow-women" may have been too unusual for the jury at the Mountain Film Festival. I was rather disappointed, and I still think it's a good film.'

Dear Marion   *28 June 1989*
I've just come off the mountain for a few days of essential rest at base camp. We've put up fixed ropes to 6900m and set up Camp II at 6500m. We're ready to go for the summit. Rhona, the expedition leader, has ordered the return porters for 15 July. If you're not going to be at Skardu until 5 July you'll have to be quick to catch us still at base camp. I want to stay on, to bury Barbara and shoot some film at Askole.

Sue Harland is going home early. I hope you meet her on your way, as she could give you some useful tips for your trek. It's very enjoyable up here and the atmosphere is excellent. The English women didn't eat the ham on the way here, so we're eating it now. I'm looking forward to seeing you and Gertrude.

Wanda

Leoneore and Marion on the march to base camp

Meanwhile Marion, Leonore and I were walking towards Concordia. Even Marion, physically unprepared though she was by any training, was not experiencing any problems, except with Leonore's high spirits and me. Wherever we went, crazy unknown Pakistanis would make us offers of marriage. Marion could easily have sold us for improbable sums but she bravely resisted all temptation, and we enjoyed the hilarity of it all.

We met several other expeditions on their way down. They all seemed unhappy with one another, glad to be getting out of the wilderness and on their way home. They questioned us incredulously. 'How could you possibly have wanted to march up here for fun?' But we were enjoying every minute. I was particularly curious to get my first

glimpse of K2, the mountain of mountains, about which I had heard so much and even written a book. Looking at photos, even the finest, had failed to fire my imagination or given me any sense of the fascinated grip in which K2 seemed to hold so many climbers. When we reached Concordia I positively ran across the glacier to see the giant face to face and try to feel its magic.

Suddenly sunlight fell on it, transforming it into a single and colossal mass of white crystal. I felt a wave of force and a mad, instinctive urge to climb on its distant ridges. Now I was captivated as so many others had been before me. Marion joined me and looked around. 'Yes, it's very pretty here, but I'd soon get tired of the mountains. I'd much rather be sitting in the garden of a wine bar drinking Heuriger. A lot more comfortable than all this cold and ice and mountain-tops.'

Meanwhile Leonore had taken up a strategic position by a snow bridge over a huge crevasse, where she was asking every climber on their way down whether they had

got to the summit, whether they had had any quarrels and if so what about. Marion had to warn her, 'If you don't stop that, someone will throw you into the crevasse. Surely you can understand that the ones who haven't made it are going to be feeling cross. Stop winding them up.'

Dear Marion   *4 July 1989*
The weather is still bad, so you can take your time. Today is the seventh successive day of snow. We're not starting home now until 22 July, which means we'll be able to spend a bit of time together at base camp. In fact our position on the mountain is not at all bad. Our high camps are set up and equipped. We've also set up store tents at Camp III and fixed ropes for Camp IV up to 7350m.

The 17 Austrians with Willi Bauer have had to give up on Hidden Peak because they only had three weeks. You'll probably meet them on their way down. The Americans also had to go home without a summit to their name although they were a brave lot. In spite

111

of the terrible conditions they got to 7600 metres. The Japanese and the Koreans are still here at base camp. I left a food parcel for you at the Gore military camp. The expeditions that have departed all left us spare food, so we're well fed. We have only two shortages. We're running out of fuel, and we're getting low on gas because we lost a lot of cartridges in an avalanche. Can you try and buy some kerosene from the army at Gore or Concordia? My idea is to go and bury Barbara from Broad Peak base camp. Some climbers have recently covered her body with stones again, but the movement of the glacier will soon undo their work. I'm hoping that Ali Chedar and your porters will help us re-bury her.

Best wishes
Wanda

At last the weather improved, but still the expedition had to wait. But as soon as the biggest avalanches had come down the women were back on the mountain to set up Camps III and IV, and climb straight on to the summit. They had just put up the last Camp IV tent at 7400m when Geraldine began to suffer from altitude sickness. Wanda went with her until she began to feel better and was

sure she would manage the rest of the descent alone, and then climbed back to join the others. 'Next day I was a bit slower than my rather younger partner Rhona Lampard, but we reached the summit, with me filming all the way up. I felt the sort of solemnity that you feel in church. I think God must live somewhere in the mountains!'

We had heard no news from the mountain, but I had a powerful feeling that Wanda was not far away on her descent, so I set out to meet her, carefully seeking out a viable route across the snow-covered glacier. With no visible trail to guide me through the icy labyrinth it required the greatest care to avoid the crevasses. When the daylight began to fade it seemed that my intuition had failed me, and I decided to head back to our camp, but I thought I should make quite sure by climbing a small ice tower.

I spied a tiny dot on the vast expanse of snow, still at least an hour away. I raced towards her as fast at the conditions would allow, stopping every now and again to climb another icy look-out to be sure that we could not pass one another unseen. We reached hailing distance in the last of the daylight; by the time we embraced it was night.

'I'm delighted you came, because it's very

Rhona Lampard on the summit

Wanda and Rhona after their summit ascent

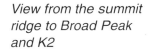

View from the summit ridge to Broad Peak and K2

◄ *The summit route follows the snow ridge on the left of the picture, up to the summit pyramid.*

of our national finances. Another problem is foreign currency, which is why we invite climbers from the West. We've also been encouraging women climbers since the 1960s, which is why our women's skills are now so far above the international average.'

Our host's patience was miraculous, as his house and even his garage disappeared under the chaos of our equipment. The walls shook with the sounds of Eric Clapton and Led Zeppelin, while the garden was transformed into a sort of Bedouin camp as we test-erected more than twenty tents. You slept where you could, on the floor. In our English *lingua franca* we called this 'carpeting'. Officially we were divided into two expeditions: the first, consisting of twelve men – from Poland, America, Germany, Austria and the Italian Tirol – bound for Gasherbrum II; the second, of five women, heading for Hidden Peak. However, Sibylle Hechtel had unexpectedly become pregnant and Kathy Murphy, from England, had returned from Mt McKinley with severe frostbite. But the absolute minimum number of climbers needed for any attempt on an 8000-metre peak is four, so a frantic search began for a fourth woman, given that Wanda was not in any circumstances prepared to settle for a man. We were lucky enough to find Shad Meena, a schoolteacher of English who was also one of Pakistan finest women climbers, but this raised another problem. The expedition was relying on the membership fees of two foreign climbers. Wanda declared that the general expedition fund could bear the extra cost, but Marek had already cut every cost he

could, and thought otherwise. Ewa was also sceptical, though for different reasons: 'I've waited a long time to get to a big summit, and I'm not prepared for teaching the basics to a Pakistani climber who's never used crampons and doesn't know the simplest rope techniques. Wanda has got to climb with Shad, and you'll partner me, won't you Gerti?' She was echoing my own concerns about Shad's participation. How could we take her money, then leave her sitting at base camp? But Wanda was not listening.

Shad Meena scraped together 5000 rupees from her modest salary as a joining fee. As Wanda pointed out: 'That's a lot of money for her, which she couldn't have raised if she weren't such an unusual Pakistani woman. It's almost impossible for a woman to live an independent life in a Muslim state, and Shad has only managed it because of her well-to-do family background.'

Wanda wanted a few days to recuperate from Makalu, and anyway needed to repair

her tents and visit a dentist, so the rest of us meanwhile flew on to Skardu.

On 1 June we packed ourselves and all our equipment into five jeeps and headed for the distant road-head. We were sharing the track with children, chickens, goats, sheep and buffaloes. Oncoming vehicles swerved out of our way at the last possible moment, and our own course was far from straight as we snaked round the potholes in the sandy track. The blare of our radios contrasted with the lines of elegant tall poplars along the irrigation canals.

We rattled on in our jeeps, bumping over huge stones, skidding in the mud and drifting through deep sand; we swayed over dizzy rope bridges and forded rushing streams between sheer brown cliffs. As we moved on from one obstacle to the next and from one breakdown to the next, the quanta of progress grew shorter and the enforced stops longer. The longest came when we became stuck in

an avalanche. The wheels of the first jeep drove deep into a mixture of snow, sand and mud, lost grip and spun. We all jumped out and pushed but the driver could manage no more than a few metres before the jeep stuck again. We spread stones liberally on the track and the driver started the engine again. Now the front wheels slid over the edge of the avalanche, the axle hit the ground and the slope back onto the track looked impossibly steep and slippery. We all held our breath until we heard a shout, 'Done it!', we looked up to see the jeep standing safe and sound beyond the avalanche with its poor engine still gasping from its exertions – which, of course, is when the next jeep stuck …

Now the valley was wider, the villages smaller and the track even more diabolical. Several times we thought our jeep would capsize, but our driver knew just what he was doing and we could see him smile at our alarm. En route we also had to select porters. Once at the road-head we began the time-

Every few hours of wilderness culminates in a village in a green oasis.

121

The trek to the Hidden Peak base camp passes directly by Gasherbrum IV.

consuming business of distributing loads and making sure they were equitable. When at last we had all the weights right it took us several more days to find the last recruits we needed. At last everything was ready and the long march could begin: through high wasteland, across endless screes and over grit-encrusted glaciers up and on towards the world's least-tamed mountains.

In these last outposts of human habitation our doctor was besieged by men and children at every night-stop. The women, of course, remained mainly invisible. The language barrier had to be overcome and the patients washed before any treatment could begin. Then examination often revealed huge suppurating sores. Often treating these wounds was less of a problem than keeping them free

from the ubiquitous dust and dirt afterwards. Many of the Baltis were suffering additionally from TB, and from chronic coughs and throat inflammations caused by the smoke in their flue-less houses.

By this time Ewa and I had become good friends and were sharing a tent. Shad Meena was finding the long daily marches very hard, but her delightful personality had won all our hearts.

Wanda caught us up at Paju, just as the porters went on strike. The village headsman at Askole had sold us a yak – which turned out to be no ordinary beast. It got up to all sorts of evil tricks, until finally it broke out of control, swam through a torrent and ran for home. Its mission had been to feed the porters and they, seeing their dinners disappear, refused to go on and demanded their pay. Since there was no way the expedition could continue without our 108 porters, Marek was bound to refuse their demands. Finally we identified the main trouble-makers and dismissed them, leaving us just 78 porters. Wanda and Marek stayed with the remaining loads, to try and recruit more porters from expeditions on their way down.

Although our two leaders Wanda and Marek were both Poles, they thought and acted so differently that they might have been from different planets. Wanda was generous by nature and would never enter into long arguments over a few rupees, whereas Marek could never forget his budget and fought and negotiated for every cent or anna.

Meanwhile the rest of us got to base camp and put up our tents on a moraine platform at the very foot of Hidden Peak, ringed by a magnificent panorama of Sian Kangri, Golden Throne and Chogolisa. The complex surfaces of the ice-fall which would be the first stage of our upward route were alive with movements of light and shade. We embraced one another, danced in delight on the moraine and installed ourselves and our belongings. At last, a settled home!

Base camp for Hidden Peak and Gasherbrum II, with Chogolisa behind

Ewa, Piotr, Leszek, Jószef and I were impatient to start setting up Camps I and II, which were to be joint for the two expeditions, and put the necessary equipment together: fixed ropes, marker poles, tents, cookers, gas cartridges, food, sleeping bags, isomats, snow anchors, ice screws and personal equipment. That meant carrying at least 20 kilos each.

At five next morning we set off towards the glacier, scraping across stones and serrated ice hummocks with our crampons. As the landscape began to take on colours in the first light of day, so also my rucksack seemed to weigh heavier with every step. We passed turquoise and lapis-lazuli ice lakes, emerald water courses and bottomless crevasses. We were not roped, which was pleasant because we could set our own pace, but dangerous. We could never be sure that this or that snow-bridge would carry our weight. Early in the day we followed marker posts set by a Japanese expedition that was attempting Hidden Peak by the south-west ridge, but we soon had to search out our own viable route through the ice labyrinth and under the constant fall of ice from the hanging glacier of Hidden Peak. We held our breath in hope and moved with all the speed we could muster.

After eight o'clock the sun would become our white-hot enemy, and the sky a cloudless, shimmering, domed vault set over heads like an incandescent fire. There was no shade for respite and what breeze there had been abandoned us. Every step was an heroic effort. When Piotr sank thigh-deep into a crevasse and the crevasses under the snow-bridges grew ever deeper, we knew the time had come to rope up.

After the ice-fall our way led up, through waist-deep soft snow. We were still on the steepest of the slope when the sun disappeared behind the mountains and the cold

Ewa with one of the heavy rucksacks to be hauled up to the high camps

more climbs to our high camps, and contemplating how near we had been to the summit. Indeed Peter Brill, Kurt Lyncke, R.D. Caughron, Marek Jósefiak, Leszek Sikora and Jószef Gozdzik from our expedition, and Claudia Carl and Wolfram Cosmus from a German expedition had got to within a few vertical metres of the summit when the snow conditions had become too dangerous for them to continue. Peter Brill and R.D. Caughron had been carrying a short rope, on which they could have reached the top, but there would have been no time to secure the whole party and the risks of a descent in darkness were too great. The two men said, 'It wouldn't have been right to take the summit on our own.' Opinions differed among our group about this stand, but I found it admirable.

Imagine our astonishment when we read a report in the mountaineering press a few months later that Claudia Carl and Wolfram Cosmus had reached the summit. I believe I owe it to all the members of our expedition to set the record straight and set down exactly what happened.

Andrej Pilz, Piotr Pustelnik and I were retreading the route between Camps I and II after a heavy snowfall. Andrej felt unwell and turned back. After a while Piotr and I, making slow progress and seeing two dots following us, thought we were about to get reinforcements. They caught us up, in the persons of Claudia and Wolfram, about half-way to Camp II. They refused to help us, but set up a store. Next day they followed us in the comfort of our footsteps and set up their Camp II next to ours; and waited for our first summit team to arrive. The highest they got was lower than our summit group. There is no basis for their claim to have reached the summit.

As the days ran out all those on the mountain had time for only one last attempt. Wanda, Ewa and two Koreans were on Hidden Peak, as were the Japanese, though on a different route; everyone else was on Gasher-

Hidden Peak from about 7000 metres on the ascent of Gasherbrum II

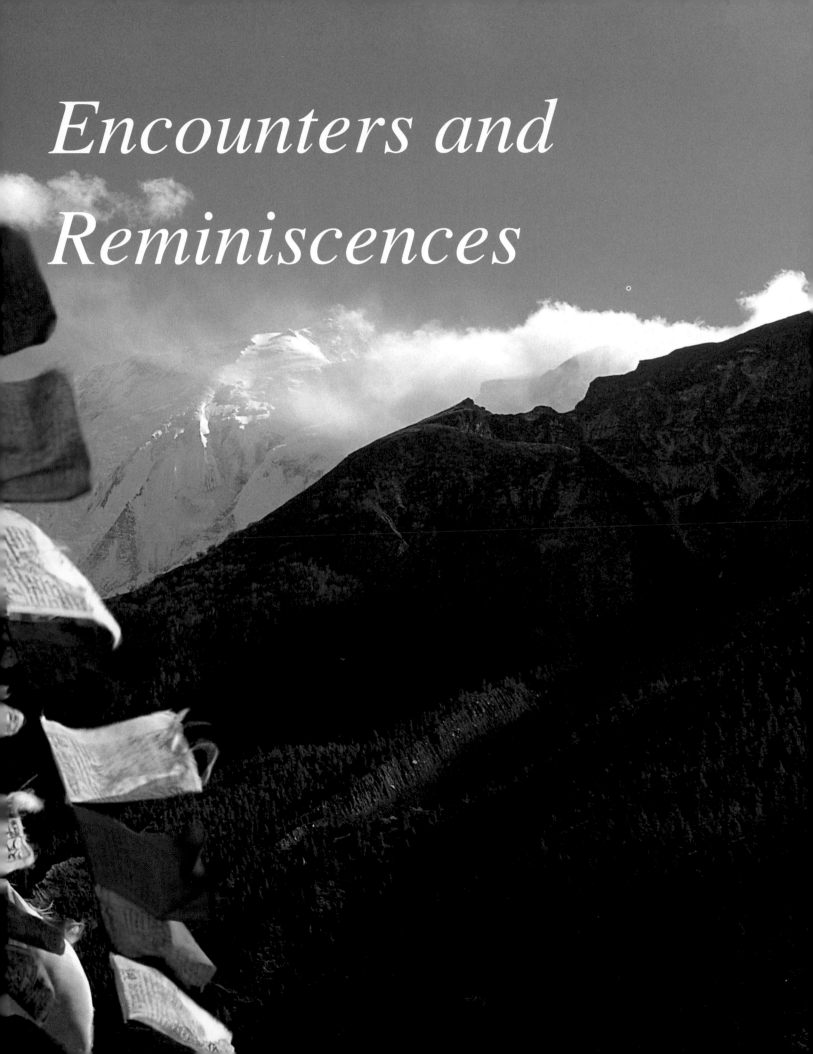

Encounters and Reminiscences

Rendez-vous
des Hautes Montagnes
at Zermatt

Among Wanda's admirers was the celebrated Swiss climber Felicitas von Reznicek, who wrote of first meeting Wanda in Zermatt in her book *From Crinoline to Grade VI*: 'Wanda Rutkiewicz came to the first Rendez-vous des Hautes Montagnes at Zermatt in 1968 with her friend Halina Krüger-Syrokomska. All the men fell for her dry charm, though no one thought she could ever become a really good climber. But she soon showed what she was made of. In 1971 she led the Danish climber Siri Melchior up the difficult 'Bayerländer Weg' on the north face of Triglav. By the time she came to the next meeting, at Andermatt in 1973, she and her team had followed in the steps of Messner and Hiebeler to record only the second ascent of the north buttress of the Eiger. In the winter of the same year, she and her three women partners secured a place in the history of the Swiss Alpine Club when they climbed the north face of the Matterhorn.

'Within a few more years Wanda was beginning to achieve the ambition she had cherished for so long, of climbing the giants of the Himalaya. She had to make many sacrifices and she invested all of her energies, her intelligence and her personality in the quest for records. Anyone who knows Wanda will understand how much her conquest of Everest means to her.'

Disappointed hopes

Wanda's second husband Dr Helmut Scharfetter was almost ten years her senior and had both professional and family responsibilities. His ways of dealing with the world were very different from hers and, for all her admiration for him, she began to feel alienated from him. Later she was to reach a better understanding of his character. 'But I don't regret having separated from him. Every passing year irrevocably changes each of us and our view of the world, so the problem of our discrepant ages would never have gone away. I'm not made for any relationship that doesn't give me space for my own personality, even if the other person's offer of his heart is sincere. I believe that there can be good relationships in which each party has freedom, but at the time I forced myself to accept something I didn't really want because I was unhappy. I'm not an easy person to live with, and both my husbands were jealous of the time I devoted to my mountain obsession and found it threatening.

'Both my husbands climbed when I first knew them, but later gave up climbing to devote themselves to their professions, whereas I was determined to continue, regardless of the problems that might arise. Maybe I shall give it up one day, but I don't think that would ever be because someone was demanding that I stop. It was my character that made my marriages fail, not the expeditions or the climbing. I mostly prefer to enjoy my experiences alone and I don't often feel a need for any close personal relationships.

'I'm a natural introvert, but I'm always being pressed to openness or self-revelation. Because I'm reticent, I'm often accused of indifference, and it was something like this conflict that led to the end of my second marriage after only three years. Helmut and I were both sad when our relationship failed and sorry to part, but our differences kept multiplying, until there was no alternative.

'All the same I was unpleasantly surprised when Helmut agreed so promptly that we should separate. Even when the judicial process was complete, we knew that there remained some emotional ties between us. I think I still felt love for him, and I believe that he still felt great affection for me too.'

Helmut Scharfetter's analysis of his time with Wanda was both soberer and more critical: 'The Wanda I first knew was an 18-year-old girl in the rather tatty clothes that were all that the first climbers allowed out of Poland could put together. There were dozens of them falling off the Dolomites at the time. I'd been taught to climb by my father, and he always insisted that he and I went to the mountains to live, not die. I often repeated this to Wanda, but there was no holding her – which was characteristic of her, and of the times. Wanda was incredibly attractive in those days, and fascinatingly intelligent. She used to come to visit a good friend of hers in Innsbruck. At that time she was a convinced communist, and she had learned to play every bit of that system to further her own long-term aims, but a time came when the ugly reality of the system forced itself upon her …

'When the Polish State of Emergency was declared, we let ourselves be pressurized into a marriage that was hasty and unconsidered. I wanted Wanda to stay in the West and she wanted her freedom of movement, which she would acquire as an Austrian citizen … My sons were very fond of Wanda, and they loved to hear her describe her adventures. I came near to persuading her to go back to computer engineering here in the West, but there was no interesting her in anything but her expeditions. She would spend whole days

and nights on the phone, planning and organizing, often shut up in her room – 'Do not disturb'. There was no chance for a loving relationship to develop, or even a partnership. It was no different on expeditions: we were competitors, not partners. She wasn't going to climb behind any man's backside! … I enjoyed climbing, but I wasn't prepared to allow it to interfere with my professional life or, worse still, become my life's only purpose.

'I soon realized that we had married in haste, and would have to separate. We were hardly ever together and were mostly engaged in quite different activities. It got to the point where Wanda never came home at all between one expedition and the next. Even then I never felt angry with her, but that's when I decided that our marriage had become pointless. No amount of tolerance could make life possible with someone like Wanda. She was an egotist, totally inconsiderate of others, and wanted only admirers around her who would unreservedly support her and work themselves to death in her causes. She even exploited her own sister Nina in Poland. Wanda could never think about anything but her current project. In theory she would have liked to possess qualities of tenderness and eroticism, but in practice, they were not part of her grand design. It was impossible to have any exchange of affection

with Wanda and, although she might regret this void in her persona, she had no way of filling it. Sex was never a deep or very mutual bond. Wanda was attracted by the idea of a husband as a kind of socially acceptable accessory. As a surgeon I qualified, though she ranked me no higher than a whole army of other possible surgeons. My intended role was to provide the colours that were missing from her own bright palette. Wanda perceived our agreed separation as a defeat, and it was not in her nature to resign herself to defeat.

'It is hard to say how much Wanda was formed by her tragic childhood. Her brother and sister are very different from her, and lead what most people think of as normal lives with families and children. Wanda was both a child of her time and a climber of her time. Mountaineering has moved on, but Wanda was a product of the Eastern bloc system of those days, which is to say that she enjoyed a lot of privileges but knew that it would take a large measure of egotism to achieve her ends. The other women that she climbed with were no different; in fact Halina, who never gave a second thought to the needs of her family or her little daughter, was perhaps even more driven than Wanda.

'Many years after we separated, Wanda wrote me a remarkable letter. It was the first time I had ever known her to express joy in the wonders of nature. Until that day the mountain had been simply the mountain – nothing more nothing less. I sometimes felt she had become a mere clothes-horse for equipment manufacturers – a role that drove her into bitter competition with what should have been her fellow expedition climbers. Her 'Caravan of Dreams' project was like jumping off a high wall: a sure recipe for the kind of death that Wanda had always wanted. The kind of expedition climbing that she knew is as dead as she is. And she could never have borne to live with herself as an ageing, unattractive ex-climber.'

A shy diva
Encounter with a superstar

I first met Wanda in 1986, after her K2 expedition. I was naturally intrigued by this Polish superstar, with her reputation for stepping casually over frozen corpses. My opportunity came at the opening of an artificial climbing wall in Munich. The real Wanda revealed herself as very different from the none too flattering legend. Here was a shy diva, carefully weighing her words to make sure that there should be no misunderstandings. I had a lawyer friend in Vienna, Dr Marion Feik, who had met Wanda several times and been fascinated. Finding it hard to believe that anyone involved at the highest levels of such an expensive activity as mountaineering should be operating without an agent or sponsors, Marion had decided to work for Wanda as her manager and agent.

I had agreed a date with Wanda for an interview the next day. She was staying with

Marion visited Wanda in her base camps as often as she could.

a friend in a high-rise apartment block. She got up in the morning, still sleepy, to walk her two dogs, and got lost on the way back to the apartment, leaving me waiting for hours. However, the interview did get going in the end, and I was treated to a riveting account of the K2 expedition.

Wanda's radiant serenity and her pleasant, quiet voice soothingly disguised some of her more dogmatic opinions, but I began to perceive the manifest contrast between the opinions and the person. I formed an impression of a restless woman torn in all directions by a host of different attitudes and passions.

Marion Feik soon became Wanda's most intimate and trusted friend and flung herself into her new role of manager and agent. She was not slow to understand Wanda's immediate needs: money, friendly attention and a nest – to look forward to while she was on expedition and to recuperate in afterwards from the physical maulings suffered on the mountains. It was Marion's achievement to bring a measure of peace and privacy into Wanda's restless life and to help her rebuild her finances – now non-existent since she had long ago spent all her savings from her

A happy day's climbing on the Hohe Wand near Vienna

*Wanda persuaded
the author to join her
on a forthcoming
expedition.*

original academic profession – from lectures, sponsors and film-making.

'Like so many others before me, I was fascinated by her aura and the sheer power of her personality. I was not a climber, so Wanda's mountain conquests didn't interest me much, but her qualities as a human being interested me very much indeed. I could see that anyone would need help who lives on the furthermost edge and almost daily encounters the death of friends, even if she is the undisputed champion among the world's top women high-altitude climbers.' Marion knew absolutely nothing about mountaineering at first, but she was quick to understand Wanda's ambitions and her needs.

It soon became clear what an exceptional person Marion Feik was, tireless in support of her precious Wanda. She nursed the vital relationships with sponsoring companies, drummed up money and equipment, and negotiated all Wanda's fees, contracts and lecture schedules. Increasingly she shaped her life to Wanda's needs, yet she never fell into possessiveness. Wanda found in Marion the only kind of friend she could accept without feeling that her liberty was threatened.

Marion lavished a mother's care on her 'prodigal foster-daughter', though Wanda was the older woman. 'There are some other notable women high-altitude mountaineers, but none of them has devoted her life so exclusively to climbing, partly because their husbands wouldn't stand for it. If you're a woman and you want to break with convention, you have to do it alone.'

Yosemite
Vacation in a climbers' paradise

In 1988 Wanda gave a number of lectures in the USA, and her films on Everest and 'Tango Aconcagua' were screened at the Telluride Mountain Film Festival. She wrote to Marion Feik:

Dear Marion   4 June 1988
I've moved on a bit. The lectures went down well – better than in Austria and Italy – and people seemed interested to talk to me. Of course I went on to Yosemite, which is a real climbers' paradise. I was pleased I could manage quite a few routes even though I hadn't trained on rock for some time. I specially enjoyed an easy route on Half Dome, done not to demonstrate my skill nor to crack a particular route, nor to notch up some summit, but just for pleasure. I partnered two

Wanda with her American climbing

nice American women who were old friends.

I hope I'll have more chances to climb like this – simply for my own pleasure. Firm rock, sunshine, light clothes and climbing shoes make a delightful change from all that expedition gear – heavy rucksack, thick clothes, with a kilo of boot and another of crampon on each foot. Not that I'm tired of the big mountains. It's one of the contradictions of life that anything you do can make you feel satisfied and dissatisfied both at the same time.

I think I've discovered that I have three reasons for climbing. First, I love being in Nature and feeling the wonder of the mountains. You can't appreciate them by looking at pictures of them at home; you have to experience the real thing. Secondly, I love climbing and I enjoy the good times with my fellow-climbers. Thirdly, I adore adventure and danger. I can't live without them.

I treasure the peace that follows on danger, and I intend to put it to constructive and creative use by writing and making films. What the general public sees in sport is the competition, so they need the competitive element in mountaineering, but when they demand the sensational, they want death and disaster, not success …

Wanda came to Vienna in October 1988 and

Wanda had last been with Arlene Blum, the leader of the expedition, on Noshaq in 1972.

Charisma and chaos
A lecture in Vienna

as usual we friends and admirers had to hang around for hours waiting for her. It was not unusual for Wanda to arrive several days late for a date or appointment. She lived too fast, took on far too much and would never say 'no' to anything. There was no keeping up with her. Her friendships had to survive on the short interstices of repose which she allowed herself only to relieve the absolute extremes of exhaustion.

Wanda had just scraped together enough money to buy a professional presentation outfit, complete with two projectors and sound mixer, to add value to her lectures. I had been producing such multivision shows for a while, so I offered to help, but Wanda would have none of it. She was determined to do everything herself, even though the time was desperately short. She just managed to put all the slides together correctly but connecting up the various machines proved more troublesome.

The lecture was to take place in the grand lecture theatre of the university in Vienna, and Wanda only arrived when the audience were already in their seats. She had so rushed the cabling that nearly every connection was wrong and virtually nothing worked properly. The images appeared in the wrong order and the fades and dissolves failed to dissolve or fade. Even worse, all the projectors projected all the time so that images stacked up on the screen like visual sandwiches. There had been no time for tests or experiments so, to save the day, the organizer and I had to cover and uncover projector lenses by hand.

I was furious. Why on earth had Wanda bought all this expensive equipment? Why on earth must she do everything herself but not leave herself time to do it properly? She could have produced a much better result with a single, simple slide projector, with less risk of the images beaming up in a chaotic, random mixture of expeditions, mountains, and family snaps. But Wanda was quite unruffled, apologized for her lateness and her technical hitches, and lectured on in her broken German as though everything were just fine. I could not believe it. Yet she held her audience with her vivid descriptions and her radical opinions:

I lust after mountains. They attract me like magnets. I never set out with the purpose of challenging death. I insist on proper equipment and proper physical preparation. I satisfy myself that I am capable of dealing with any possible problem on my own, even in the dark or the worst of weathers. This still leaves some risk, but that is the essence of adventure. We never live more fully or better appreciate our life than when we risk losing it …

Wanda in a losing battle with technology

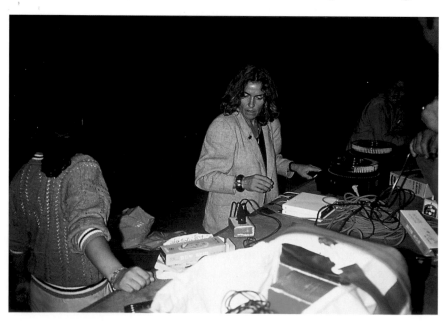

146

... Do you know, I admire the wives of celebrated mountaineers more than I admire the men themselves. What man would agree to lead their lives? Climbers are not like other humans and it is difficult for them to find compatible partners. I can not resist the mountains, and that is why I have chosen the single life. My delight is to know the world, feel the joy of standing on its peaks, expand my store of experience, and expand in the excitement and the emotions and the energy of expedition communities. I best love my life when it is at its most dramatic and replete ...

... I don't feel driven to be the best, but I do seek challenge. I compete with myself. I set myself new targets and new tests of my capacities every time I embark on a new expedition. There is nothing extraordinary about climbing an 8000-metre peak. Many women could do it, given the organization and the will-power; which is not to say that anyone could get to the top of the very highest mountains. There is a difference between climbing as a hobby and performance climbing, and these peaks are not for the hobbyist. This is doubly true of alpine-style climbing, which demands intensive training. With every year that passes more and more tourists are coming to trek in the Himalaya who have never climbed at home, and I fear that these ill-prepared visitors will be tempted to emulate the real climbers, to their own great peril and that of others ...'

Little of this idealized wish-list bore any relation to the facts. In truth Wanda now had no time to train and her poor equipment lay where she had abandoned it in Kathmandu, Delhi and Islamabad. Anything that broke had to be mended there and then, and she often forgot what she had left where.

By the end of the lecture I realized that I could never hope to change Wanda's personality. She would always do everything herself, regardless of the outcome, and she would never be able to accept help from any-

one but Marion, who had been honoured with an unique place in Wanda's life.

More and more Wanda was living in a world of her own, with its own rules that no one else could hope to understand, and those rules certainly did not require her to change the manner of her lectures. Wherever she went, it was the same chaos, but also the same fascinated attention from the audience, and never mind the pictures.

Members of the Neukirchen Alpine Club in Upper Austria have memories of a lecture at Wels on 7 October 1988. The projectors packed up completely and the audience began to whistle. Wanda's quiet response was, 'Look, I grew up on goat's milk, so this kind of thing really doesn't bother me ...'

The committee made sure that a technician was hired for Wanda's lecture at Neukirchen. The first of her lectures at which everything worked was at Katowice – and it was to be her last lecture.

The third Raichle Adventure Prize, in recog-

Milestones in the history of women's climbing

History claims that the nun Aetheria from Aquitaine climbed Mount Sinai in 385 AD. Katharina Botsch and Regina von Brandis were the first recorded all-women team when they climbed the Laugenspitze in the Italian Tirol together in 1552. Medieval Europe believed that the mountains were the home of spirits and devils. A girl in Davos who climbed the Tinzenhorn was accused of witchcraft and burned at the stake. In 1809 a group of young men from Chamonix dragged a French woman, Marie Paradis, to the summit of Mont Blanc in order to exhibit her for money at fairs. In 1856 the Empress Elisabeth was prevented from going beyond the foot of the glacier because it was thought unseemly for a lady to climb further.

It was an Englishwoman, a Mrs Cole, who after greatly enjoying excursions on the Monte Rosa and Mont Blanc in 1859 assured the ladies of England that they too might make excursions in the Alps with great pleasure and few inconveniences. Another Englishwoman, Lucie Walker, who climbed the Matterhorn in 1871, went on to climb many more of the 4000-metre peaks in the Alps and is regarded as the first serious woman mountaineer.

British women climbers founded their Ladies' Alpine Club in 1907 because the British Alpine Club refused them membership – and continued to do so until 1975! The Swiss Alpine Club was no different: founded in 1863, but women excluded until 1978. The women responded by founding their own club in 1918. There are still some local sections of the Swiss Alpine Club that exclude women, in marked contrast to the Swiss Friends of Nature, who have accepted women and men alike since the day their association was formed in 1895. When Paula Wiesinger-Steger (now 88 years old) won the World Ski Championships in 1932, she was nicknamed 'The Mad Woman of Bolzano'. Partnered by her husband, she was the first woman to climb the Preuss crack on the Cima Piccola. Four years later she was guiding and leading climbers. In those days good skiers were also good climbers. It was an American, Miriam O'Brien who, in 1927, first declared that no one who never led but always followed could ever hope to become a real climber. She and her partner Alice Damesme made alpine history in 1932 as the first women's rope to climb the Matterhorn.

Women were beginning to explore parts of the Himalaya from about 1850. Cenzi von Ficker-Sild, having been given the mountain Ushba as a present by a Caucasian prince, joined with others to climb it. The women's altitude record was held for many years by a Massachusetts women's rights activist, Fanny Bullock Workman, who travelled the Himalaya with her husband between 1890 and 1915. Her main rival was Ernie S. Peck, a New England schoolteacher who launched her climbing career at the age of 45 by climbing the Matterhorn, and in 1908, aged 58, as the first climber to conquer Huascaran South (6656m) in the Peruvian Andes. Another exceptional adventurer, the Frenchwoman Alexandra David-Neel, went to the Himalaya at the age of 55, dressed herself as a Tibetan beggar and walked 2000 miles to the forbidden city of Lhasa. Her travels on the Tibetan plateau and over several high passes of the Himalaya still count as one of the most remarkable explorations of all time.

In 1934 Hetty Dyhrenfurth was a member of the expedition that explored the Baltoro glacier in the Karakorum, when she also reached the summit of Queen Mary Peak (7428m) and set a new altitude record for women. Loulou Boulaz and Lulu Durand were the next to carry the baton. Boulaz made the second ascent of the Croz buttress of the Grandes Jorasses on Mont Blanc in 1935, became World Ski Champion in 1936 and 1937, was the first woman to scale the Walker Buttress in 1952, but was baulked four times on the north face of the Eiger by bad weather. Daisy Voog was the first woman to succeed on the North Face, in 1964.

An international women's expedition to Cho Oyu in Nepal was the first all-women team to attempt an 8000-metre peak, and cost the lives of its leader Claude Kogan – considered to be the world's finest woman climber – Claudine van der Stratten and Ang Norbu in an avalanche. Claude Kogan had made the first ascents of Salcantay in 1952, Nun Kun in 1953 and Ganesh Himal in 1955, and had taken over the women's altitude record during her first attempt on Cho Oyu in 1954.

Written accounts exist of a number of English and Scottish women's expeditions which reached 6000-metre peaks without loss of life or injury. The first success for a women's expedition on an 8000-metre peak came in 1974 when three Japanese reached the summit of Manaslu. The first woman to the top of Everest – Junko Tabei, also Japanese – reached the summit on 16 May 1975, to be followed on 27 May that year by the Tibetan Phantong. When Wanda Rutkiewicz stood on the summit on 16 October 1978, she was the first European woman to succeed. Junko Tabei collected a second 8000-metre peak – Shisha Pangma – in 1981. In 1985 Wanda Rutkiewicz led the first women's team to reach the top of Nanga Parbat, and in 1986 she was the first woman ever to the top of K2. In 1987 she added Shisha Pangma to her successes, which were finally to include also Gasherbrum II, Hidden Peak, Cho Oyu and Annapurna for a total of eight 8000-metre peaks

Women are still under-represented in the alpine sports, but their equality in pure climbing has never been disputed. Lynn Hill, Corinne Labrune and Isabelle Patissier notched up a string of universally-recognized successes, and Catherine Destivelle has soloed the Eiger north wall in winter. The record of women climbers on the world's 8000-metre peaks is impressive:

1974   Manaslu (8163m), three Japanese climbers; Mount Everest (8848m), Junko Tabei, Japan

1975   Gasherbrum II (8035m), Halina Krüger-Syrokomska, Poland

1978   Annapurna (8091m), Vera Komarkova and Irene Miller, USA

1981   Shisha Pangma (8046m), Junko Tabei, Japan

1982   Dhaulagiri (8167m), Lutgaarde Vivijs, Belgium; Hidden Peak (8068 m), Marie-José Valençot, France

1983   Broad Peak (8047m), Krystyna Palmowska, Poland

1984   Cho Oyu (8201m), Vera Komarkova, USA and Dina Sterbova, Czechoslovakia: Nanga Parbat (8125m), Liliane Barrard, France

1986   K2 (8616m), Wanda Rutkiewicz, Poland

1990   Makalu (8463m), Kitty Calhoun, USA

1996   Lhotse (8516m), Chantal Mauduit, France

1998   Kanchenjunga (8595m), Ginette Harrison, UK

International conference of the adventure élite

'Montagna Avventura 2000' was the title of a conference held in Tuscany from 11 to 14 December 1989, to which adventurers were invited from all over the world, including Wanda, Walter Bonatti and Krzysztof Wielicki, who also brought Celina Kukuczka, the widow of the great Polish mountaineer Jerzy Kukuczka. The whole event was dedicated to the memory of Kukuczka, who had perished on the south face of Lhotse earlier in the year, on 24 October.

Wanda delivered a paper, in which she set out what adventure meant to her.

Krzysztof Wielicski, Celina Kukuczka and Wanda

Freedom is central to my life and it is in the mountains that I seek my freedom. In the mountains my gender is irrelevant; what matters is to be among friends. Adventure can reawaken our primal instincts and lead us back to Nature. When we survive in the mountains it is by conquering our own weaknesses, not by conquering Nature. In fact we have a duty to Nature: to liberate our natural environment from its domination by our species.

It is not easy to practise what we preach when we are at 8000 metres and suffering from oxygen deficiency, but we must try to remember what we believe and impose some rules on ourselves even when we are at the limits of our capacities. Here are some suggestions. Never carry more on to the mountain than we can carry off again. Carry away all detritus. Keep good equipment and re-use it on our next expedition. Do not engage porters primarily to provide home comforts: use their help to keep the mountains clean. Go to the mountains and the open spaces for love, not to fight. That would be a better gift to future generations than our conquests of peaks, and I would enthusiastically support

any project that could give us this cleaner world.

In future I propose to invite groups of trekkers to accompany my expeditions, to help me clear up the garbage from my own expedition and from previous groups. It is far easier to persuade climbers and trekkers of the need to protect the environment than to convince ministries and agencies for tourism in developing countries, fearful as they are of losing revenues or being forced to invest. It is my sincere hope that as many as possible of my fellow-climbers may support my blueprint for a cleaner mountain wilderness.

The Karakorum is a long way from, say, the Dolomites, but more and more climbers are heading for the Himalaya. Our world is shrinking and cheap air travel is bringing the remotest places within reach of huge numbers of people. But the majority are not travelling in search of adventure and many of them are quite unaware of environmental problems of any kind.

'Living your dreams, instead of just dreaming them, is not without risk.'

I hope that our species may achieve a better relationship with its environment, though my experience leaves me less than hopeful. It need not matter how many or how few go to the mountains. What will count is how they behave when they get there. Nor do I believe that any lectures I give or films I distribute are likely to draw more tourists into the hills, if only because I select my content with care. My lectures have a purpose, which is to illustrate my arguments with images. As for those whose love is for Nature and the mountains, they have an absolute right to escape from the stresses of their ordinary lives and pursue their quest for peace.

The world has changed since the days of my first expeditions. Today visitors swarm to India, Nepal, Pakistan and Tibet, and although they do not actually destroy any-

thing, yet still their leavings pollute the environment and their very presence is changing the lives and the customs of the true inhabitants. Agriculture is being neglected because trekkers and expeditions pay better and, though it may be beyond us to reverse these developments, we should nevertheless try to turn them to some more positive direction. If the leaders of these countries continue to sell off the mountains lock, stock and barrel, as though they were a mere commodity, the mountains and their communities will be irrevocably destroyed, Unfortunately this is not yet well understood. It is only natural that they should want the money, to buy their way out of national poverty. For us, from more fortunate lands, not to visit would be no remedy: it is already too late. However, there are all sorts of ways for us to demonstrate

152

our consideration for our hosts. For example, it should hardly need saying that we should photograph and film only at the express invitation of local people. Respect for individuals will rightly be seen as respect for the community.

Today, if you are rich enough, it is as easy to book an expedition to an 8000-metre peak as a package tour. The mountains are easier to get to and dreams of climbing on them are easier to realize. However, more people on the peaks do not make them less dangerous, or easier to climb, or warmer. Oxygen starvation, rock-falls, avalanches, storms and extreme pitches make no distinction between amateurs and professionals on the mountain. The death zone is still as deadly as ever.

It is obvious that expedition members must be capable of looking after themselves, but on commercial tours this self-sufficiency often sinks to such indifference of one member for another that you can see tour climbers pass one another without even exchanging a word. The weak can be just as selfish – I am tempted to say immoral – as the strong, but in other ways. They arrive on the mountain without even the most basic training or preparation for what they intend. Then they wait until others have done the serious work of fixing ropes and establishing camps before venturing their own summit attempt. And then they go home to boast of their stolen victories.

Every year the commercial tours to the Himalayan peaks and other great mountains of the world cost the lives of many of their clients. Those who pay may lack experience, or be too pressed for time, or acclimatize too quickly, or be too ambitious, or overestimate their skills, or be too obsessed with the summit as their only goal. I am not suggesting that the normal routes to the 8000-metre peaks have become routine. Who would dare say so and belittle what are still extraordinary achievements? Each and every individual who gets to those tops and returns alive has demonstrated an exceptional measure of

alpine skills, and been blessed with good fortune. But official reports emphasize the successes and pass over the failures, while the media limit their reporting to spectacular disasters. An expedition that runs smoothly is not news.

We have set new records. We have climbed extreme routes. Both men and women representing dozens of the world's nations have stood on our highest peaks. But ... and here let me quote Sir Edmund Hillary: 'The number of climbers at the highest levels has grown enormously. Most of them command superlative and modern technique on rock and ice. They do unbelievable things in the Alps and Yosemite. But they nearly all make the mistake of thinking that their exceptional skills are sufficient for the Himalaya and similar mountains. In doing so they ignore the many unique problems such as altitude, cold, distance from base, weather and, most importantly, avalanches.'

Let me conclude. It is of the essence of adventure that the outcome depends on many more elements than merely my own skills, and that is why I enjoy every expedition and every climbing excursion as an adventure. This international adventure conference gives us an opportunity to study the problems of adventure and join together in the search for solutions. Thank you for having allowed me to share my views with you.

What marks out adventurers? Are their lives faster and more intense?

1991–1992

1991	Awarded Sitara-i-Imtiaz Order of the Republic of Pakistan for outstanding mountaineering achievement; second attempt on Kanchenjunga; Cho Oyu (8201m); Annapurna (8091m)
12 May 1992	Disappears on Kanchenjunga

The Caravan
of Dreams

The south face of Annapurna from base camp

other expedition members and had not had time to strike up any new friendships, but that was because of my own decision to attach myself to an expedition of relative strangers and climb with instant partners. I've no doubt that they would have tried to help if the need had arisen, though I don't know what, as things stood, they could have done. On the steep face I had three safe staging posts, but I was in much greater danger once I reached the more open terrain. Once again it was up to me to master those irrational fears that still take hold of me when I'm climbing alone, and especially when I'm alone at night. I have a vivid memory from my failed attempt on Broad Peak. I set out from a high camp about midnight, knowing that I would have to skirt a crevasse with the dead body clearly visible in it of a climber who had been hurled down by an avalanche into what had become his grave. I could hardly bring myself to keep going. I can't explain these kinds of fear. Why should we be frightened of the dead? Perhaps extremes of exertion play havoc with our reason and fill our heads full of nonsense.

I made good progress, although I wasn't feeling very good. Early on 22 October, a little above Camp III, I met Riszard on his way down and asked him about the route to the summit. An obvious question which, to my surprise, Riszard hesitated to answer, perhaps because he was nervous that I might use the information to support a fraudulent claim that I had got to the top. This was a problem I had never encountered before, and I could hardly believe my ears. I had heard of other climbers who had been deeply offended when they had been doubted in similar circumstances. On the other hand it is true that cheats do exist who are prepared to claim successes that never happened. In the end Ryszard did tell me, with a very bad grace, that I should look out for old fixed ropes. When I was about 100 metres below the summit and saw Rüdiger coming down, the general direction was clear. Where the ice face

168

This girl is hauling home a gigantic sheaf of rice straw.

of the summit dome gets steeper and steeper I found the fixed ropes leading up to the almost vertical snow ridge that joins the two summits, with the main summit to my left. I just had time to see how close I was to my goal before the summit disappeared into a cloud. I felt a great happiness. I was not quite alone. I could see two other lone climbers ahead of me; the first reached the summit at noon, the second at 3 in the afternoon.

I reached the summit about sunset. Taking photographs was rather a problem, first because I was unsteady on my injured leg, secondly because it meant taking off my gloves and thirdly because the light was failing. The valleys were already in darkness, but I managed to get some shots of the surrounding peaks before the shutter on the camera froze and I had to give it a good shake to release it. I assumed that there'd be nothing on that negative and I was really cross. Also there was nowhere to set up my tripod for a time-release picture and the whole business was getting too complicated in the icy wind. I didn't feel like raising base camp on the radio. I preferred just to stand quietly and drink in the beauty of the mountains in the darkening night.

On the way down I missed my route by a few hundred metres in spite of the bright moonlight, and got on to some very steep ice slopes where it was hard to stay on my feet in

the high wind. Worse still, my head lamp wasn't working. Now I was really frightened. I knew I had only two alternatives: the near certainty of a fatal fall from where I was, or to climb back up again to more level ground. So up I struggled to 7800m and dug a bivouac platform on a little snow ridge.

I spent quite a pleasant night in my bivouac bag, followed by an easy descent the next day, by which time a following group was already on its way to the summit. I radioed to base camp from Camp II where I spent the next night. Wielicki later cited my failure to radio from the summit as proof that I never reached the summit. He claimed to have watched me through binoculars and seen me turn round short of the summit and he added, for good measure, that I couldn't be relied on to remember what I'd done because I had probably been suffering from

The Annapurna-South-Face team

altitude sickness. There must be gaps in my memory, he said, and I must have been hallucinating. The message was: 'To be pronounced sane, the lunatic must first admit to having been mad.'

What a nasty business! I think it is the worst experience I've had in all my years of climbing. In the end Krzysztof was prepared to retreat a little, but only to say: 'If you say you reached the summit, I shan't contradict you, but personally I don't believe it.'

The rest of my descent was a nightmare. The pain in my leg was so bad that I thought that I must have broken it again. It seemed inconceivable that I could have reached the top on it, but obviously climbing up must have put less strain on the muscle than coming down. When I got to the bottom of the fixed ropes I couldn't find my ski sticks. Either someone had taken them, or they had simply sunk into the ice. That made things even worse because it meant that I couldn't take the weight off my leg. When I had to jump the bergschrund the agony was so unbearable that I burst into tears out of sheer pain and loneliness. It took me two days to drag myself and my heavy rucksack with every bit of my gear from the mountain down to base camp.

I couldn't afford to leave anything because my plan depended on a quick departure to catch my next expedition. I radioed base camp with a request for some help, but no one came, and in fact many of the other team members had already gone home. Apart from our Nepalese, only Bogdan was still there and he was slightly ill. Or at least he was claiming to be so, having been told by Wielicki that I should have stayed at base camp to nurse my bad leg and therefore had only myself to blame. My injury hadn't stopped me from going up, so what was to stop me coming down by myself. He may have been right, but what had become of common humanity? We had come here as friends and now we were parting more like angry wolves from rival packs.

I had now climbed eight 8000-metre peaks, just as he had, and perhaps that is what had turned our relationship so hostile. He wanted to believe that this route, one of the most difficult in all the Himalaya, had been beyond me ... but I did it, and I did it alone. You can't really take photos of one another when there's only one of you. In the end, it was all very unpleasant.

The summit route was very impressive, very dangerous and more difficult even than my route on K2. It is lucky that Annapurna is not so high. I was delighted to have succeeded in spite of my problems, but sorry to have been granted so few of the pleasures of friendship. But I suppose I should be getting used to that. If only Ewa could have come the whole adventure might have been a joy. But I'm not saying it was a bad expedition. The others were nice and there were plenty of laughs. The quarrel was entirely between Wielicki and me; Bogdan is a serious young man who, unfortunately, let himself be influenced on this occasion.

As you can imagine, I wasn't much looking forward to my return to base camp. I didn't think I'd be getting three rousing cheers on

The climb on the south wall of Annapurna is considered to be one of the hardest routes of the Himalaya. Wanda's ascent was the first by a woman.

171

The north face of Dhaulagiri, with its 'Eiger'. The expedition was aborted and had left base camp before Wanda could get there.

Wanda's rucksack, jettisoned every piece of gear that was not absolutely essential, and refilled the bag only with the rest. However, as they climbed higher, the ever-increasing danger of avalanches forced them to turn back before even reaching base camp.

It was the disappointment of her ambitions on this expedition that finally persuaded Wanda never again to involve herself in the organization of a venture, but always to join existing expeditions as an independent associate. 'What makes me very sad is that I don't have any real partners any more. Ewa

Pankiewicz can only come very occasionally, for all sorts of professional and family reasons, even if I pay for her. And the same sort of difficulties apply to several of my other favourite partners …'

It bothered Wanda that Polish climbers claimed to be too poor to mount expeditions because they themselves could not afford all the costs. She observed that Western climbers were not much better endowed to carry such costs themselves, but routinely depended on sponsors. 'It's not impossible to find sponsors in Poland. Why should we expect something for nothing just because we're Poles? I don't think that's a very constructive attitude.'

Wanda's original plan to climb all eight of her remaining peaks in the course of that one year had now become an impossibility. She had no choice but to extend her timetable to the spring of 1993. 'I think that's possible. I want to break a record by going straight from one mountain to the next; but if it turns out to be feasible, I'd like to include some difficult routes rather than keep tramping the normal summit approaches. In my book mountaineering is sport not leisure – and it can stir feelings and emotions that even transcend sport.'

Wanda's 'Caravan of Dreams' had turned into a more formidable organizing challenge than she had ever foreseen. On the one hand it had proved impossible to organize an actual caravan moving on from one mountain to the next; but on the other hand, keeping her progression moving through paid member-

ship of a series of different expeditions not only required careful co-ordination, but could founder any time that an expedition might be cancelled.

When Spring 1992 came and Wanda was still six peaks short of her goal with only a few months of her timetable left, I thought that she might actually admit defeat in her crazy race against time. But of course I was wrong.

Meanwhile Marion's task was to search out expeditions that would be going to Wanda's eight mountains and to organize paid places on them. Wanda by now cared neither whether she knew the other members, nor what routes they had chosen. Only two things mattered. Could she raise the fee in time? And would the expedition accept her? Marion had little idea of the dangers inherent in Wanda's chosen way. Indeed she preferred not to know, but simply to make her own contribution to the possible fulfilment of the dream.

The snow was so deep that Wanda and Arek never even reached base camp.

Heavy snowfalls meant that every part of the path had to be trodden afresh day after day.

Dear Marion   2 May 1992

Nothing is going according to plan. We're sitting at base camp, waiting for the helicopter to lift Elsa and Alfredo to have their frost-bite treated. We've been foiled by the weather. Snowstorms and thunderstorms all at the same time – and at this altitude. Can you believe it? It was all quite an adventure. I was at the tail end of a group climbing to set up Camp IV at 7900m. Suddenly the weather turned, there was no visibility, and I lost Elsa, Carlos, Arek and Alfredo. I was carrying my sleeping bag and my Gore-Tex bivouac bag so I decided to bivouac on my own. I was quite safe but I was a bit fearful of what might happen the next day. In the morning the wind dropped and I found the others only 100 metres above me, so there was no chance of our getting higher than Camp IV. The first thing I heard when I reached them was that Arek was feeling ill

and was going to turn back, which he did there and then. He had been working particularly hard the day before. The others had also had a bad night and were out looking for a better site for their tents. I think my bivouac bag may be the better bet.

Love Wanda

The Kanchenjunga expedition had been ill fated right from the start. Of the six members, four had had to drop out because of illness or injury. Only Wanda and Carlos were left to make a final attempt on the summit. The date was 7 May.

The flashing light told me that there was a message on my answering machine. Marion's voice rang out, sobbing: '… Wanda's dead! I've just had Arek on the phone from Nepal …' I wrestled on my own with the news for several days, stunned, devastated, yet not feeling able to speak to anyone, least of all Marion. We had all known that this moment would come one day, but we had all suppressed our fears. It was just as Wanda had so often said: 'Climbers are masters of denial.'

Wanda Rutkiewicz went missing on 12 May on Kanchenjunga, the third-highest of her fourteen giants. Marion was still receiving her last letters long after Wanda's life had ended – the last of a much richer correspondence than she had ever received from previous expeditions. Was this a bad sign? Or was she leading up to some new plan? However that might have been, Marion's final letter from Nepal came from Carlos.

High camp in the shelter of an ice cleft

Dear Marion   27 May 1992
I want to share my grief at Wanda's death with you, and Wanda's family, and with all her friends. As Arek has told you, there was nothing we could have done. I waited for her at 8000m, and again at Camp II, until I was certain she couldn't still be alive. There was simply no way of mounting a rescue operation. I didn't simply abandon her after I had met her at 8300m. She was cold, but in full command of her faculties, and she was determined to go on to the summit. I couldn't dissuade her, even though she was very tired and had no sleeping bag, no cooker, no water and no food. We don't know whether she died in her bivouac cave or on her way up to the summit or on her way down; all we know is that she is gone for ever. We feel so sad and so sorry, but there was nothing we could have done. I'm quite certain that she couldn't have committed suicide because I know how much she loved life. We loved Wanda!

By the end of the expedition Wanda and I were the only ones still capable of attempting the summit, but Wanda was much slower and I couldn't wait for her. We were all together until 7 May, when Arek was forced to turn round by a fever and stomach pains; and

Andres had to follow the next day. Wanda and I started out from Camp I on 9 May and made good progress. We reached Camp II that day and Camp III – which we found in ruins – the next day. Now the snow was very deep and our progress much slower. Wanda bivouacked whereas I went on to the ice cave where we had Camp IV. The weather was so bad the next morning that I had to sit out the day. A very tired Wanda joined me, with the bad news that her cooker was not working. We melted some snow, ate and drank until our gas had run out, and then slept for a few hours. Wanda had slight diarrhoea. At 3.30 the next day, 12 May, the weather was fine and we set out again. Wanda was moving slowly, which was not surprising since it was almost impossible to keep upright on a layer of snow covering solid ice. Above the ice pinnacles the snow was even deeper and I soon lost sight of Wanda. I got to the summit at 5 in the afternoon and I saw Wanda again on my way down. She was sitting under an overhanging rock, and she said she would wait until the next day to go for the summit. I waited for three days in Camp II, but she never came; so I left a fully-equipped tent for her and climbed down to base camp. On 21 May,

179

Advanced base camp at the foot of the north wall

when the weather deteriorated again, we left base camp. Wanda's death is a terrible loss to us all, but especially to the mountaineering community. Deciding to leave the mountain was very hard, but we knew that she couldn't have survived in such terrible weather.   Carlos

On 28 October Austrian TV organized a memorial meeting and a press conference, and it was here that Carlos Carsolio and Arek Gasienica-Jozcowy reconstructed the likely course of Wanda's last climb:

The first summit attempt, on 23 April, failed in bad weather. Wanda was moving slowly but she suffered no frost-bite.

The second attempt began with Carlos and Wanda climbing together to Camp III. On the way from there to Camp IV Wanda bivouacked in an ice cave at 7400m, while Carlos continued to Camp IV, arriving there about 6 next morning. Wanda arrived that evening, very tired, complaining of diarrhoea, and with her cooker not working.

The next morning they roped up, set out at 3.30 a.m. and climbed very slowly together to the col in deep snow lying over smooth ice. At the col they unroped and Carlos fought his way to the top through the deep snow on the summit ridge.

On his descent Carlos found Wanda in a snow cave at 8300m, exhausted and trembling with cold. She had her bivouac bag, but no sleeping bag and no cooker. She had drunk all her water and asked Carlos for something to drink, but he had nothing either. Nor could he offer her anything more to wear because he was equally lightly equipped and was himself suffering from the extreme cold.

Wanda was adamant in her determination to reach the summit, and only enquired what difficulties remained. Carlos gave her details of the two couloirs and the 20 metres of unstable rock just below the summit. She said she was glad to have Carlos's footprints to guide her, and she was very excited. Finally she sent Carlos on his way with a cheerful,

181

It was all so different

'When I look down I see a world rushing for-wards, mindless of where or why. I see people fighting and tearing one another and I under-stand neither their purposes nor their rea-sons. I have less and less to say to them; more and more I keep silence.'

Wanda's mother is 86 and the likeness between mother and daughter is astonishing. When she moves or makes a gesture the illu-sion is of the living Wanda. 'I should like to

Wanda with her mother

see Wanda's huge achievements recognized and honoured. She was warm-hearted, always full of sympathy for anyone having a hard time and she never spoke ill of others. She was generous; she loved giving presents to her friends, but she hardly ever received anything in return, except from Kukuczka and Messner. Messner, especially, was always a stout supporter, and she never ceased to be grateful to him. Other so-called friends exploited her or even cheated her, but she could never bring herself to express her deep disappointment. It's amazing how rarely she displayed real anger or bore

grudges, even though she so often helped others to bear the burden of their unhappi-ness. Things happen on the mountain that you dare not talk about. After those horrible events on Annapurna she had no option but to go on to Kanchenjunga. The atmosphere in Poland had become so poisoned with hatreds and jealousies that she could not bear to come back here. She needed to go some-where better. Wanda was always a creature of hope. She and I thought alike and she knew that she could only hope to find good things and brighter horizons in the hills, not down here. I once went on to the rock with her and although the climbing terrified me, I can understand her passion.

'When Wanda was little I came from Lithuania to Poland with my husband in search of a better life than we could hope for in our divided native land. Then came Com-munism and bad times everywhere; but it would have done no good to go under. We were happy and we were strong because we lived and supported one another as a family, even after her father was no longer with us. Wanda was never just an athlete. She was so good at Russian that she earned money trans-lating Russian poetry. I'm happy that things are improving in Poland and we all have a better life. My husband's pension, which he worked so hard to earn, is enough for me to live comfortably, and anyway my needs have always been modest. I have everything I want and I feel quite at home in Wanda's apartment.

'Whenever Wanda was about to leave for an expedition, I used to go round to her apart-ment and bless her. She was always in a great rush, surrounded by packing chaos. I never felt afraid for her; I had a feeling that nothing bad would happen to her, and she always promised not to take silly risks.

'But when she was leaving for Kanchenjunga, it was all so different. Her apartment was all neat and orderly. And Wanda nearly slipped away without my having drawn the sign of the Cross on her forehead. I had to call out after her, and she seemed almost reluctant to come back. It was not the same. It was as though she were hiding something from me, as though she had plans. When her climbing companions came to tell me that she was dead, I said: "No. I know that she's alive, but in a better place where she is happy." She sometimes visits me in the night, and when she touches me I am lifted on a wave of strength and energy. She gives out silver rays which fill me with a great joy when they shine on me, and they hold me to life. She has set me one last task: to live, by the strength she gives me, for as long as she needs me here. Wanda's love embraced all of mankind.'

185

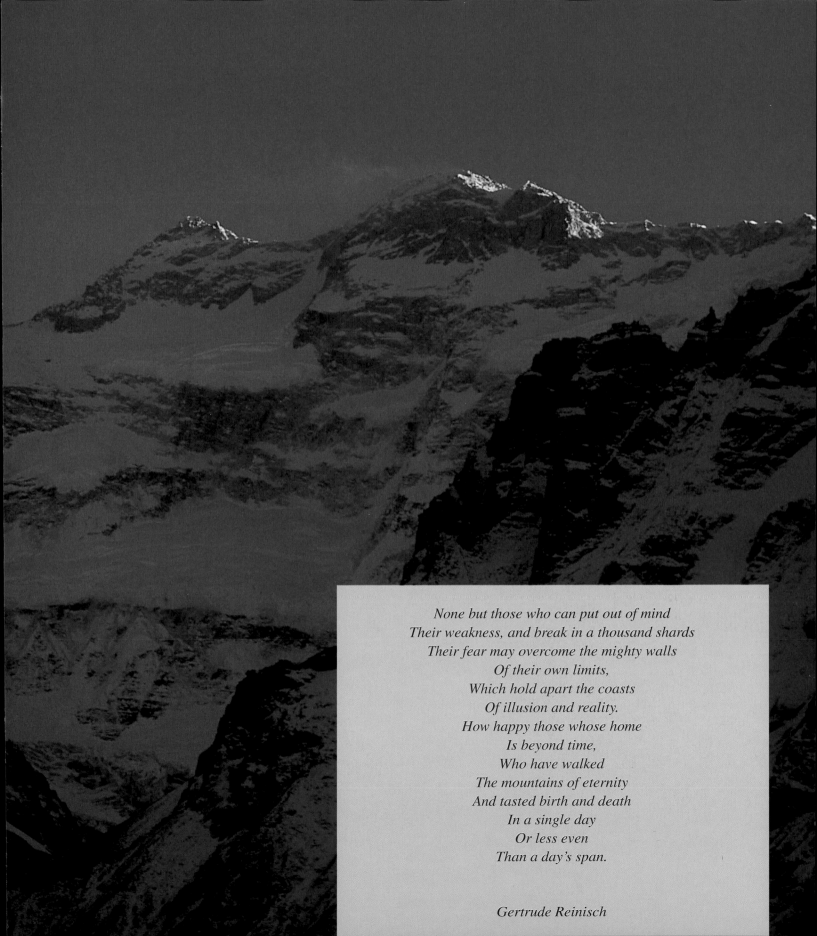

None but those who can put out of mind
Their weakness, and break in a thousand shards
Their fear may overcome the mighty walls
Of their own limits,
Which hold apart the coasts
Of illusion and reality.
How happy those whose home
Is beyond time,
Who have walked
The mountains of eternity
And tasted birth and death
In a single day
Or less even
Than a day's span.

Gertrude Reinisch

Reference

Sources

Letters and personal communications from family, friends and acquaintances; television, newspaper and magazine interviews; documentary and reportage film material

Numerous books and journal articles, particularly expedition accounts by other leading mountaineers, mostly in German, but including also, in English,

Bill Birkett and Bill Peascod, *Women Climbing,* The Mountaineers, 1990

Arlene Blum, *Annapurna,* Orac Pietsch 1982 **and**

Himalayan Mountaineering Journal, vol. x, 1975–76

The full list of sources can be found in the original German edition of this book published by Bergverlag Rother, Munich

Films, books and honours
Films

Wenn Du zu dieser Wand kommen würdest? (Join me on these rocks)

Requiem – 1986, K2 expedition

Tango Aconcagua

Abenteuer am Shisha Pangma (Adventure on Shisha Pangma) – with Jerzy Kukuczka

Karneval am Fuße des Cerro Torre (Carnival at the foot of Cerro Torre)

Schneefrauen (Snow Women) – 1989, Gasherbrum II

Books

Two books with Ewa Matuszewska and one with Barbary Rusowicz – all in Polish (listed in the original German edition of this book published by Bergverlag Rother, Munich)

Honours

Six Polish national honours for exceptional sporting achievement

Graz Film Festival prize for the film Requiem

1982 Rolex Enterprise Award
1988 Raichle Adventure Prize
1989 Victor de l'aventure, France
1990 Match d'or, Paris
 Minerva della donna, Italy
1991 Sitara-i-Imtiaz Order of the Republic of Pakistan for outstanding mountaineering achievement

The climbing decades

1964 Mnich, north-east wall, Variant R, High Tatra
1967 Mont Blanc group, Grépon east wall and Grands Charmoz
1968 Trollryggen, east buttress (V), Norway: first women's expedition
1970 Pik Lenin (7134m), Pamirs
1971 Triglav, north-east wall, Bayerländer Weg, Julian Alps
1972 Noshaq (7492m), Hindu Kush
1973 Eiger, north buttress – second ascent, first by a women's team
1974 Attempt on Pik Korshenevskaya (7105m), Pamirs – reaching 7000m
1975 Gasherbrum III (7952m), Karakorum – expedition leader, highest ever first ascent by a woman
1976 Attempt on Nanga Parbat – reaching 6500m
1978 Matterhorn, winter ascent of north wall – first winter ascent by a women's team
 Mount Everest (8848m), Himalaya – third ascent by a woman, first by a European woman and first by any Polish climber, male or female
1979 Grand Capucin, east wall by Bonatti route – women's team
 Petit Dru, west wall 'Directe americaine' – women's team
1981 Elbrus, Caucasus – complex fracture of the leg, followed by 21/2 years on crutches
1982 K2 – women's expedition member and leader, approach march to base camp on crutches
1984 Attempt on K2 – women's expedition, reaching 7400m
1985 Aconcagua (6959m), south face, Andes – climbed alpine style
 Nanga Parbat (8125m), Himalaya, Kinshofer route on the Diamir face – first women's team, expedition leader
 Second attempt on Broad Peak – reaching 7800m
1986 K2 (8616m) by Abruzzi Ridge – first woman and first Pole
 Third attempt on Broad Peak
 Attempt on Makalu (8463m) – reaching 8000m
1987 Winter attempt on Annapurna (8091m) – reaching 7000m
 Shisha Pangma (8046m), Himalaya – first Polish climber
1988 Yosemite
 Winter attempt on Yalung Kang, Kanchenjunga group, Himalaya
1989 Gasherbrum II (8035m), Karakorum – women's team

1990 Second attempt on Makalu Hidden Peak (8068m), Karakorum

1991 Second attempt on Kanchenjunga (8586m), Himalaya Cho Oyu (8201m), Himalaya, west face from Tibet – solo ascent Annapurna (8091m), south face, Himalaya – solo ascent, first ascent by a woman

1992 Third attempt on Kanchenjunga – reaching c. 8300m

Wanda's 8000ers

1978 Mount Everest (8848m), Himalaya – third ascent by a woman, first by a European woman and first by any Polish climber, male or female

1985 Nanga Parbat (8125m), Himalaya, Kinshofer route on the Diamir face – first women's team, expedition leader

1986 K2 (8616m) – first woman and first Pole

1987 Shisha Pangma (8046m), Himalaya – first Polish climber

1989 Gasherbrum II (8035m), Karakorum – women's team

1990 Hidden Peak (8068m), Karakorum

1991 Cho Oyu (8201m), Himalaya, west face from Tibet – solo ascent

1991 Annapurna (8091m), south face, Himalaya – solo ascent, first ascent by a woman

Captions to the panoramic illustrations

Cover and pp. 2/3: Gasherbrum II – Camp II

p. 1: Wanda after her successful ascent of Gasherbrum II

pp. 4/5: Gasherbrum II (right) and Gasherbrum III (left)

pp. 6/7: Makalu base camp

pp. 8/9: Full moon at Annapurna base camp

pp. 12/13: Kanchenjunga massif with Jannu from the North-west

pp. 14/15: Mnich (Monk) from Morskie Oko

pp. 20/21: Mont Blanc du Tacul, Grand Capucin and ridge du Diable from Glacier du Géant

pp. 40/41: Baltoro Glacier – Concordia

pp. 138/139: Annapurna group from the North

pp. 154/155: Lower summits of the Kanchenjunga massif from the West

pp. 186/187: Last of the sunshine on the north face of Kanchenjunga

pp. 188/189: In the heart of the Kanchenjunga group

Gertrude Reinisch is a journalist, the author of several books and a qualified alpine mountain leader. She lived for three years in various regions of the Himalaya, where she climbed many 6000-metre peaks. Since her first encounter with Wanda Rutkiewicz, she has recorded many additional mountaineering achievements.

1986 First meeting with Wanda;

1987 Mountain bike trek – more than 3000km – throughout Tibet;

1990 Member of Wanda Rutkiewicz's Polish expedition to Hidden Peak (reaching 6600m) and of Marek Grochowski's to Gasherbrum II (reaching 7800m);

1991 Mount McKinley, Alaska

1994 Organizer and leader of the first Austrian women's expedition – in memory of Wanda Rutkiewicz – to Shisha Pangma (8046m), five members reaching the summit;

1995 Wanda Rutkiewicz Memorial Trek to Kanchenjunga – and production of a documentary video;

1996 Austrian expedition to Gya, an unexplored region of the Indian Himalaya – and production of a documentary video.

'I have a passionate love of every kind of mountaineering – including ski touring, rock climbing and ice climbing.

'The experiences and incredible - adventures that I was allowed to share as a member of the Polish - expedition to Gasherbrum II have deeply influenced my view of the world. They have given me the confidence to jettison some of the safety nets of my previous life and conquer the worst of my existential fears; and the grandeur of Nature, my unwavering confidence in my Polish colleagues and my own emotional highs all combined, during those memorable days, to push me to achievements to which I could never have aspired before.'